MASTERING PYTHON FOR AI AND DATA SCIENCE

Practical Techniques and Hands-On Projects to Boost Your Skills in Artificial Intelligence

THOMPSON CARTER

TABLE OF CONTENTS

INTRODUCTION 14

WHY THIS BOOK? 14

WHAT WILL YOU LEARN? 15

WHO IS THIS BOOK FOR? 16

THE BIGGER PICTURE: WHY AI MATTERS..................................17

HOW TO USE THIS BOOK 18

LET'S GET STARTED..19

CHAPTER 1: PYTHON FUNDAMENTALS FOR AI 20

CHAPTER 2: WORKING WITH DATA: LIBRARIES AND TOOLS 28

1. INTRODUCTION TO NUMPY 28

2. INTRODUCTION TO PANDAS 30

3. INTRODUCTION TO MATPLOTLIB 32

4. INTRODUCTION TO SEABORN 34

5. PUTTING IT ALL TOGETHER 35

CHAPTER 3: PYTHON FOR BIG DATA................................37

1. THE CHALLENGES OF BIG DATA 37

2. INTRODUCTION TO DASK 37

3. HANDLING BIG DATA EFFICIENTLY 39

4. COMPARING DASK TO PANDAS 40

5. USE CASE: PROCESSING LARGE DATASETS 40

6. SCALING BEYOND A SINGLE MACHINE 42

7. ADDITIONAL TOOLS FOR BIG DATA IN PYTHON 43

8. PRACTICAL EXAMPLE: COMBINING PANDAS AND DASK 43

CHAPTER 4: SETTING UP YOUR AI WORKSPACE...................45

1. SETTING UP PYTHON ENVIRONMENTS 45

2. CHOOSING AN IDE OR CODE EDITOR.......................................46

3. INSTALLING ESSENTIAL LIBRARIES AND TOOLS 48

4. CONFIGURING YOUR WORKSPACE FOR EFFICIENCY 50

5. OPTIMIZING FOR LARGE-SCALE AI PROJECTS..........................51

6. TESTING AND DEBUGGING TOOLS 52

7. PRACTICAL EXAMPLE: YOUR FIRST AI WORKSPACE SETUP................53

CHAPTER 5: VERSION CONTROL WITH GIT 55

1. WHY USE VERSION CONTROL FOR AI PROJECTS?....................55

2. INSTALLING AND SETTING UP GIT..55

3. BASIC GIT COMMANDS 56

4. COLLABORATING WITH GITHUB 58

5. BRANCHING AND MERGING 59

6. HANDLING CONFLICTS 60

7. ADVANCED GIT FEATURES..60

8. WORKFLOW FOR AI PROJECTS 62

9. PRACTICAL EXAMPLE: COLLABORATIVE AI PROJECT..............63

10. INTEGRATION WITH AI TOOLS 64

CHAPTER 6: DATA CLEANING AND PREPROCESSING 66

1. THE IMPORTANCE OF DATA CLEANING..66
2. HANDLING MISSING DATA 66
3. SCALING AND NORMALIZATION..69
4. ENCODING CATEGORICAL VARIABLES..70
5. FEATURE TRANSFORMATION 71
6. AUTOMATING DATA CLEANING..72
7. PRACTICAL EXAMPLE: DATA CLEANING WORKFLOW 73

CHAPTER 7: EXPLORATORY DATA ANALYSIS (EDA).............76

1. IMPORTANCE OF EDA..76
2. STEPS IN EDA..77
3. UNIVARIATE ANALYSIS...78
4. BIVARIATE ANALYSIS...79
5. MULTIVARIATE ANALYSIS 80
6. OUTLIER DETECTION 81
7. FEATURE RELATIONSHIPS AND INSIGHTS 82
8. AUTOMATING EDA 83
9. PRACTICAL EXAMPLE: EDA WORKFLOW..84

CHAPTER 8: INTRODUCTION TO STATISTICS FOR AI.........86

1. IMPORTANCE OF STATISTICS IN AI 86
2. TYPES OF STATISTICS 86
3. KEY STATISTICAL CONCEPTS 87
4. PROBABILITY IN AI 89

5. HYPOTHESIS TESTING 90

6. CORRELATION AND REGRESSION 91

7. ADVANCED TOPICS 92

8. PRACTICAL EXAMPLE: STATISTICAL INSIGHTS FOR AI 93

CHAPTER 9: FEATURE ENGINEERING AND SELECTION ...95

1. IMPORTANCE OF FEATURE ENGINEERING AND SELECTION 95

2. FEATURE ENGINEERING TECHNIQUES 96

3. FEATURE SELECTION TECHNIQUES 98

4. AUTOMATING FEATURE SELECTION 100

5. PRACTICAL EXAMPLE: FEATURE ENGINEERING AND SELECTION
WORKFLOW 101

6. BEST PRACTICES 103

CHAPTER 10: WORKING WITH TIME-SERIES DATA 104

1. UNDERSTANDING TIME-SERIES DATA 104

2. LOADING AND INSPECTING TIME-SERIES DATA 105

3. PREPROCESSING TIME-SERIES DATA 106

4. ANALYZING TIME-SERIES DATA 107

5. FORECASTING WITH TIME-SERIES DATA 108

6. ADVANCED TECHNIQUES 110

7. EVALUATING MODEL PERFORMANCE 111

8. PRACTICAL EXAMPLE: FORECASTING WEBSITE TRAFFIC 112

CHAPTER 11: SUPERVISED LEARNING FUNDAMENTALS ..114

1. INTRODUCTION TO SUPERVISED LEARNING 114

2. LINEAR REGRESSION 114

3. LOGISTIC REGRESSION 117

4. COMPARING LINEAR AND LOGISTIC REGRESSION 120

5. PRACTICAL EXAMPLE: PREDICTING STUDENT PASS/FAIL 120

6. BEST PRACTICES 121

CHAPTER 12: TREE-BASED MODELS 123

1. DECISION TREES 123

2. RANDOM FORESTS 125

3. BOOSTING TECHNIQUES 126

4. XGBOOST 127

5. COMPARING DECISION TREES, RANDOM FORESTS, AND XGBOOST .128

6. HYPERPARAMETER TUNING 129

7. PRACTICAL EXAMPLE: PREDICTING CUSTOMER CHURN 130

8. BEST PRACTICES 131

CHAPTER 13: UNSUPERVISED LEARNING AND

CLUSTERING 133

1. INTRODUCTION TO CLUSTERING 133

2. K-MEANS CLUSTERING 134

3. DBSCAN (DENSITY-BASED SPATIAL CLUSTERING OF APPLICATIONS

WITH NOISE) 135

4. HIERARCHICAL CLUSTERING 137

5. EVALUATING CLUSTERING PERFORMANCE 138

6. COMPARING CLUSTERING ALGORITHMS 140

7. PRACTICAL EXAMPLE: CUSTOMER SEGMENTATION 140

8. BEST PRACTICES 141

CHAPTER 14: DIMENSIONALITY REDUCTION TECHNIQUES...143

1. IMPORTANCE OF DIMENSIONALITY REDUCTION 143

2. PRINCIPAL COMPONENT ANALYSIS (PCA)...144

3. T-DISTRIBUTED STOCHASTIC NEIGHBOR EMBEDDING (T-SNE).........146

4. COMPARING PCA AND T-SNE 147

5. EVALUATING DIMENSIONALITY REDUCTION.......................................148

6. PRACTICAL EXAMPLE: CUSTOMER SEGMENTATION 149

7. BEST PRACTICES 150

CHAPTER 15: NATURAL LANGUAGE PROCESSING (NLP)...152

1. INTRODUCTION TO NLP 152

2. TEXT PREPROCESSING 153

3. SENTIMENT ANALYSIS 155

4. WORD EMBEDDINGS 157

5. PRACTICAL EXAMPLE: ANALYZING PRODUCT REVIEWS 158

6. BEST PRACTICES 160

CHAPTER 16: UNDERSTANDING NEURAL NETWORKS 161

1. ANATOMY OF A NEURAL NETWORK 161

2. FORWARD PROPAGATION 162

3. BACKPROPAGATION..163

4. STRUCTURE OF A NEURAL NETWORK..164

5. BUILDING A NEURAL NETWORK IN PYTHON.............................165

6. PRACTICAL EXAMPLE: PREDICTING BINARY OUTCOMES...................167

7. BEST PRACTICES...168

CHAPTER 17: BUILDING DEEP LEARNING MODELS WITH TENSORFLOW AND PYTORCH 170

1. INTRODUCTION TO TENSORFLOW AND PYTORCH 170

2. SETTING UP TENSORFLOW AND PYTORCH 171

3. BUILDING MODELS WITH TENSORFLOW................................171

4. BUILDING MODELS WITH PYTORCH 172

5. COMPARING TENSORFLOW AND PYTORCH.............................174

6. PRACTICAL EXAMPLE: MNIST DIGIT CLASSIFICATION.................175

7. BEST PRACTICES...178

CHAPTER 18: CONVOLUTIONAL NEURAL NETWORKS (CNNS)..180

1. WHAT ARE CONVOLUTIONAL NEURAL NETWORKS? 180

2. ARCHITECTURE OF CNNS..181

3. BUILDING A CNN WITH TENSORFLOW/KERAS 182

4. BUILDING A CNN WITH PYTORCH 184

5. OBJECT DETECTION WITH CNNS.......................................187

6. BEST PRACTICES FOR CNNS...187

CHAPTER 19: RECURRENT NEURAL NETWORKS (RNNS)..189

1. WHAT ARE RNNS?..189

2. ANATOMY OF AN RNN..190

3. CHALLENGES WITH RNNS..191

4. ADVANCED RNN ARCHITECTURES...................................191

5. BUILDING RNNS WITH TENSORFLOW/KERAS...................192

6. BUILDING RNNS WITH PYTORCH.....................................193

7. NLP APPLICATIONS WITH RNNS......................................194

8. BEST PRACTICES FOR RNNS..196

CHAPTER 20: TRANSFER LEARNING AND PRE-TRAINED MODELS..198

1. WHAT IS TRANSFER LEARNING?......................................198

2. PRE-TRAINED MODELS..199

3. TRANSFER LEARNING WORKFLOW...................................200

4. TRANSFER LEARNING FOR IMAGE CLASSIFICATION............201

5. TRANSFER LEARNING FOR NLP..203

6. PRACTICAL EXAMPLE: FINE-TUNING BERT FOR SENTIMENT ANALYSIS..205

7. BEST PRACTICES FOR TRANSFER LEARNING.....................205

CHAPTER 21: GENERATIVE MODELS AND GANS................207

1. WHAT ARE GENERATIVE MODELS?...................................207

2. WHAT ARE GANS?..208

3. HOW GANS WORK..208

4. BUILDING GANS WITH TENSORFLOW/KERAS...................209

5. APPLICATIONS OF GANS...213

6. Variations of GANs 213

7. Best Practices for Training GANs 214

8. Challenges with GANs 214

CHAPTER 22: REINFORCEMENT LEARNING BASICS 216

1. What is Reinforcement Learning? 216

2. The RL Workflow 217

3. Types of RL Approaches 217

4. Markov Decision Process (MDP) 218

5. Q-Learning 218

6. Deep Reinforcement Learning (Deep Q-Learning) 221

7. Applications of Reinforcement Learning 224

8. Best Practices for RL 224

CHAPTER 23: AI FOR COMPUTER VISION 226

1. What is Computer Vision? 226

2. Key Technologies in Computer Vision 227

3. Advanced Application 1: Face Recognition 227

4. Advanced Application 2: Medical Imaging 229

5. Challenges in Computer Vision Applications 232

6. Best Practices 233

CHAPTER 24: AI FOR RECOMMENDATION SYSTEMS 235

1. What is a Recommendation System? 235

2. Collaborative Filtering 236

3. CONTENT-BASED FILTERING 238

4. HYBRID MODELS 239

5. DEEP LEARNING FOR RECOMMENDATION SYSTEMS...........241

6. EVALUATION METRICS 242

7. CHALLENGES IN RECOMMENDATION SYSTEMS....................242

8. BEST PRACTICES...243

CHAPTER 25: EXPLAINABLE AI (XAI)....................................245

1. WHAT IS EXPLAINABLE AI (XAI)?...245

2. CHALLENGES OF INTERPRETABILITY 246

3. TYPES OF INTERPRETABILITY 246

4. TECHNIQUES FOR XAI...247

5. APPLICATIONS OF XAI 250

6. BEST PRACTICES FOR XAI...251

7. LIMITATIONS OF XAI...252

CHAPTER 26: DEPLOYING AI MODELS 253

1. IMPORTANCE OF AI MODEL DEPLOYMENT 253

2. PACKAGING MODELS FOR DEPLOYMENT................................254

3. DEPLOYMENT WITH FLASK 255

4. DEPLOYMENT WITH FASTAPI...256

5. CONTAINERIZATION WITH DOCKER 258

6. DEPLOYMENT BEST PRACTICES 259

7. REAL-WORLD DEPLOYMENT EXAMPLE...................................260

CHAPTER 27: END-TO-END AI PROJECT: PREDICTING CUSTOMER CHURN 262

1. UNDERSTANDING CUSTOMER CHURN PREDICTION 262
2. DATA COLLECTION AND PREPROCESSING...263
3. MODEL TRAINING...264
4. DEPLOYMENT WITH FLASK 265
5. ENHANCING THE MODEL 267
6. SCALING THE DEPLOYMENT 268
7. MONITORING AND MAINTENANCE 268

CHAPTER 28: FINAL CAPSTONE: AI FOR SOCIAL GOOD.....270

1. PROJECT IDEA: PREDICTING AIR QUALITY FOR PUBLIC HEALTH 270
2. WORKFLOW 271
3. DATA COLLECTION 271
4. DATA PREPROCESSING 272
5. MODEL TRAINING...273
6. DEPLOYMENT 274
7. BUILDING A DASHBOARD 275
8. RECOMMENDATIONS FOR PUBLIC HEALTH 276
9. SCALING AND MONITORING...277
10. SOCIAL IMPACT..277

Introduction

Artificial Intelligence (AI) is no longer a distant dream of futuristic science fiction—it is now an integral part of our daily lives, reshaping industries, solving complex problems, and enhancing human potential. From the personalized recommendations on our favorite streaming platforms to life-saving medical diagnoses and automated financial systems, AI has become a transformative force, pushing the boundaries of what technology can achieve.

This book, *Mastering AI for the Real World*, is a comprehensive guide to understanding, developing, and applying AI solutions across diverse domains. With a focus on practical, hands-on learning, this book aims to bridge the gap between theoretical concepts and real-world applications. Whether you're a student, a budding data scientist, or a seasoned professional looking to upskill, this book is designed to equip you with the tools and knowledge needed to thrive in the AI-driven future.

Why This Book?

AI is evolving at an unprecedented pace, but with its rapid growth comes complexity. Many resources on AI are either highly technical, alienating beginners, or oversimplified, leaving professionals wanting more depth. This book strikes a balance by offering jargon-free explanations of core concepts, practical examples, and hands-on projects that cater to learners at different levels.

Key features of this book include:

- **Structured Learning Path:** Divided into logical sections, the book covers AI fundamentals, data science essentials, advanced machine learning, and real-world deployments.
- **Practical Projects:** Each chapter includes real-world case studies and hands-on projects to reinforce learning.
- **Focus on Social Good:** Beyond profit-driven applications, the book emphasizes how AI can address societal challenges like healthcare, education, and environmental sustainability.

What Will You Learn?

This book provides a deep dive into the AI lifecycle, starting from foundational concepts and progressing to advanced topics. Here's a glimpse of what you'll discover:

1. **AI Fundamentals:** Understand the building blocks of AI, including machine learning, deep learning, and neural networks. Learn how these concepts form the backbone of modern AI systems.

2. **Data Science Essentials:** Explore techniques for data cleaning, preprocessing, and visualization. Grasp the critical role data plays in training accurate and reliable AI models.

3. **Machine Learning and Deep Learning:** Develop proficiency in supervised, unsupervised, and reinforcement learning techniques. Master advanced topics like natural language processing, computer vision, and generative models.

4. **AI Deployment:** Learn how to deploy AI solutions using tools like Flask, FastAPI, and Docker. Discover best practices for scaling and monitoring AI systems in production environments.

5. **Ethical AI Development:** Address the pressing issues of bias, transparency, and fairness in AI. Understand how to build ethical systems that prioritize societal well-being.

6. **AI for Social Good:** Delve into capstone projects focused on solving real-world problems, such as predicting air quality for public health or enhancing disaster response systems.

Who Is This Book For?

This book is tailored for:

- **Beginners:** If you are new to AI, this book provides a solid foundation with clear explanations and beginner-friendly examples.

- **Data Scientists and Engineers:** For those already familiar with AI, the book offers advanced topics, practical projects, and insights into deployment and scalability.

- **Decision-Makers and Enthusiasts:** Professionals looking to understand how AI can be strategically applied in their organizations or fields.

The Bigger Picture: Why AI Matters

The potential of AI extends far beyond automation and convenience. AI is a tool for innovation, a catalyst for progress, and a means to address some of humanity's most pressing challenges. From improving healthcare accessibility to mitigating climate change, AI has the power to create a positive impact on society when used responsibly.

However, with great power comes great responsibility. The rise of AI brings ethical dilemmas, from data privacy concerns to algorithmic bias and job displacement. As practitioners and consumers of AI, it is our collective duty to navigate these challenges thoughtfully, ensuring that AI benefits everyone equally.

This book not only equips you with technical skills but also encourages you to think critically about the implications of AI. By combining practical expertise with ethical considerations, you will be prepared to create AI systems that are not just powerful but also responsible and inclusive.

How to Use This Book

Each chapter is designed to be standalone, allowing you to focus on areas of interest or follow the book sequentially for a complete learning experience. The book is divided into several parts:

- **Part 1: Foundations of AI** – Establish a strong understanding of AI concepts and tools.
- **Part 2: Data Science Essentials** – Learn the critical role of data in AI systems.
- **Part 3: Advanced AI Techniques** – Dive deeper into machine learning and deep learning methodologies.
- **Part 4: Real-World Applications** – Explore case studies and examples in business, healthcare, and beyond.
- **Part 5: Deployment and Scalability** – Master the art of deploying and scaling AI models for real-world use.
- **Part 6: Ethical AI and Social Good** – Understand the ethical challenges of AI and how to use it for societal benefit.

- **Part 7: Capstone Projects** – Apply your knowledge to hands-on projects solving real-world problems.

Let's Get Started

By the end of this book, you will not only understand how AI works but also be equipped to design, develop, and deploy AI systems that make a difference. Whether your goal is to innovate in business, contribute to societal well-being, or simply learn a transformative technology, this book is your gateway to mastering AI for the real world.

Let's embark on this journey together, where technology meets purpose, and the possibilities are limitless. Welcome to *Mastering AI for the Real World*.

Chapter 1: Python Fundamentals for AI

Overview

Python is the foundation of many AI and data science applications due to its simplicity, extensive libraries, and active community. This chapter will cover the essential building blocks of Python, ensuring you have a solid grasp of the language's basics before diving into advanced AI and data science topics.

---

1. Why Python for AI and Data Science?

- **Simplicity and Readability:** Python's clean syntax reduces the learning curve, allowing you to focus on solving problems rather than syntax.
- **Extensive Libraries:** Libraries like NumPy, Pandas, Matplotlib, and TensorFlow make Python indispensable in AI.
- **Community Support:** A vast community of developers contributes to resources, tutorials, and open-source tools.
- **Portability:** Python runs seamlessly across platforms like Windows, macOS, and Linux.

---

2. Installing Python and Setting Up Your Environment

- **Installation:** Walkthrough of installing Python from python.org.
- **IDEs and Editors:**
  - *Integrated Development Environments (IDEs):* PyCharm, Jupyter Notebook, and VS Code.
  - *Text Editors:* Sublime Text, Atom.
- **Package Management:** Introduction to pip and virtual environments for managing dependencies.

3. Core Programming Concepts

a. Python Syntax and Basics

- Writing and running your first Python script.

```python
print("Hello, AI World!")
```

- Python's indentation-based structure.
- Keywords and identifiers.

b. Variables and Data Types

- Variable assignment and dynamic typing:

```python
```

```
x = 10       # Integer
y = 3.14     # Float
z = "Python AI" # String
```

- Built-in data types:
    - Numbers (int, float, complex)
    - Strings (str)
    - Booleans (bool)
    - Containers (list, tuple, set, dict)

c. Input and Output

- Taking user input and displaying output:

python

```
name = input("Enter your name: ")
print(f"Welcome to AI, {name}!")
```

d. Operators

- Arithmetic: +, -, *, /, //, %, **
- Comparison: ==, !=, >, <, >=, <=
- Logical: and, or, not

---

4. Control Flow Statements

a. Conditional Statements

- Syntax for if, elif, and else:

python

```python
age = 20
if age < 18:
    print("Underage")
elif age == 18:
    print("Welcome to adulthood")
else:
    print("Adult")
```

b. Loops

- ***For Loops:***

python

```python
for i in range(5):
    print(i)
```

- ***While Loops:***

python

```python
count = 0
while count < 5:
    print(count)
    count += 1
```

c. Break and Continue

- Controlling loop execution:

python

```python
for num in range(10):
    if num == 5:
        break  # Exit loop when num is 5
    print(num)
```

---

5. Working with Functions

a. Function Definition

- Writing reusable code:

python

```python
def greet(name):
    return f"Hello, {name}"
print(greet("AI Enthusiast"))
```

b. Lambda Functions

- Inline functions for small tasks:

python

```python
square = lambda x: x ** 2
```

```python
print(square(4))  # Output: 16
```

c. Scope and Global Variables

- Local vs global variables:

python

```python
global_var = "Global"

def access_global():
    global global_var
    global_var = "Modified Global"
```

---

6. Introduction to Data Structures

a. Lists

- Creating and manipulating lists:

python

```python
fruits = ["apple", "banana", "cherry"]
fruits.append("orange")
print(fruits)
```

b. Dictionaries

- Key-value pairs for structured data:

python

```
person = {"name": "Alice", "age": 25}
print(person["name"])  # Output: Alice
```

c. Sets and Tuples

- Unordered collections (sets) and immutable sequences (tuples):

  python

  ```
  unique_items = set([1, 2, 2, 3])
  fixed_values = (1, 2, 3)
  ```

---

7. Error and Exception Handling

- Identifying and handling errors gracefully:

  python

  ```
  try:
      result = 10 / 0
  except ZeroDivisionError:
      print("Cannot divide by zero!")
  ```

---

8. Python Best Practices

- Writing clean, readable code.
- Using comments and docstrings.

- Following PEP 8 guidelines for code style.
- Documenting code effectively.

---

9. Practical Example: Data Analysis Starter Code

- A beginner-friendly example to demonstrate real-world relevance:

python

```python
import pandas as pd

# Create a sample dataset
data = {"Name": ["Alice", "Bob", "Charlie"], "Age": [25, 30, 35]}
df = pd.DataFrame(data)

# Display dataset
print(df)
```

By the end of this chapter, readers will have a robust understanding of Python's basics, empowering them to progress confidently into AI and data science topics.

Chapter 2: Working with Data: Libraries and Tools

Overview

Data is the cornerstone of AI and data science. Python provides powerful libraries like **NumPy**, **Pandas**, **Matplotlib**, and **Seaborn** to handle, analyze, and visualize data efficiently. This chapter offers an introduction to these libraries, with hands-on examples to get you started.

---

1. Introduction to NumPy

NumPy (Numerical Python) is a library for numerical computing that excels at handling large, multi-dimensional arrays and performing mathematical operations.

Key Features:

- Fast operations on arrays and matrices.
- Support for mathematical functions like mean, standard deviation, etc.
- Seamless integration with other libraries like Pandas and Matplotlib.

Getting Started with NumPy

- **Installation:**

  bash

  pip install numpy

- **Creating Arrays:**

  python

  ```python
  import numpy as np

  # Creating a 1D array
  arr = np.array([1, 2, 3, 4, 5])
  print(arr)

  # Creating a 2D array
  matrix = np.array([[1, 2], [3, 4]])
  print(matrix)
  ```

- **Basic Operations:**

  python

  ```python
  arr = np.array([1, 2, 3])
  print(arr + 5)      # Add 5 to each element
  print(arr * 2)      # Multiply each element by 2
  print(arr.mean())   # Compute the mean
  ```

- **Use Case: Data Normalization**

python

```
data = np.array([100, 200, 300])
normalized = (data - data.min()) / (data.max() - data.min())
print(normalized)
```

---

2. Introduction to Pandas

Pandas is a library for data manipulation and analysis. It provides data structures like **DataFrame** and **Series** for handling structured data.

Key Features:

- Powerful DataFrame object for tabular data.
- Easy handling of missing data.
- Efficient data filtering and grouping.

Getting Started with Pandas

- **Installation:**

  bash

  ```
  pip install pandas
  ```

- **Creating DataFrames:**

  python

```python
import pandas as pd

# Creating a DataFrame
data = {"Name": ["Alice", "Bob", "Charlie"], "Age": [25, 30, 35]}
df = pd.DataFrame(data)
print(df)
```

- ## Reading and Writing Data:

python

```python
# Read CSV
df = pd.read_csv("data.csv")

# Save DataFrame to CSV
df.to_csv("output.csv", index=False)
```

- ## Basic Operations:

python

```python
# Filter rows
print(df[df['Age'] > 25])

# Add a new column
df['Score'] = [90, 80, 85]
print(df)

# Grouping data
grouped = df.groupby('Score').mean()
```

```
print(grouped)
```

- **Use Case: Missing Data Handling**

python

```
df = pd.DataFrame({"A": [1, 2, None], "B": [4, None, 6]})
df.fillna(0, inplace=True)
print(df)
```

---

3. Introduction to Matplotlib

Matplotlib is a data visualization library used to create static, interactive, and animated plots.

Key Features:

- Flexible plotting tools.
- Support for a wide range of plot types (line, bar, scatter, etc.).

Getting Started with Matplotlib

- **Installation:**

bash

pip install matplotlib

- **Basic Plotting:**

python

```python
import matplotlib.pyplot as plt

# Line plot
x = [1, 2, 3, 4]
y = [10, 20, 25, 30]
plt.plot(x, y)
plt.title("Line Plot")
plt.xlabel("X-axis")
plt.ylabel("Y-axis")
plt.show()
```

- **Bar and Scatter Plots:**

python

```python
# Bar plot
plt.bar(['A', 'B', 'C'], [10, 20, 15])
plt.show()

# Scatter plot
plt.scatter(x, y, color='red')
plt.show()
```

- **Use Case: Data Trends Visualization**

python

```python
import numpy as np
```

```
x = np.linspace(0, 10, 100)
y = np.sin(x)
plt.plot(x, y, label="Sine Wave")
plt.legend()
plt.show()
```

---

4. Introduction to Seaborn

Seaborn is built on top of Matplotlib and provides a high-level interface for drawing attractive and informative statistical graphics.

Key Features:

- Built-in themes for professional-looking plots.
- Support for statistical plots like histograms and heatmaps.

Getting Started with Seaborn

- **Installation:**

  bash

  pip install seaborn

- **Creating Visualizations:**

  python

  import seaborn as sns

```
# Simple histogram
data = [1, 2, 2, 3, 3, 3, 4]
sns.histplot(data, bins=4)
plt.show()
```

```
# Heatmap
matrix = [[1, 2], [3, 4]]
sns.heatmap(matrix, annot=True)
plt.show()
```

- **Use Case: Data Relationships**

  python

```
tips = sns.load_dataset("tips")
sns.scatterplot(data=tips, x="total_bill", y="tip", hue="sex")
plt.show()
```

5. Putting It All Together

A complete example showcasing NumPy, Pandas, Matplotlib, and Seaborn for analyzing and visualizing data:

python

```
import numpy as np
import pandas as pd
import matplotlib.pyplot as plt
import seaborn as sns
```

```python
# Generate sample data
data = np.random.randint(10, 100, size=(10, 2))
df = pd.DataFrame(data, columns=["Feature1", "Feature2"])

# Data analysis
df['Sum'] = df['Feature1'] + df['Feature2']

# Visualization
plt.figure(figsize=(10, 6))
sns.barplot(data=df, x=df.index, y="Sum")
plt.title("Feature Sum Visualization")
plt.show()
```

By mastering NumPy, Pandas, Matplotlib, and Seaborn, you will gain the essential tools needed to manipulate, analyze, and visualize data effectively. These libraries form the foundation of AI and data science workflows, enabling you to uncover insights and present findings in a meaningful way.

Chapter 3: Python for Big Data

Overview

Handling large datasets efficiently is a critical skill in AI and data science. Python's versatility, combined with libraries like **Dask**, empowers you to work with datasets that exceed memory constraints while maintaining high performance. This chapter explores how to process, analyze, and manipulate big data efficiently.

---

1. The Challenges of Big Data

- **Volume:** Large datasets may not fit into memory, causing performance bottlenecks.
- **Variety:** Data can come in structured (tables) or unstructured (logs, images) formats.
- **Velocity:** Processing data in real time requires optimized tools and techniques.
- **Veracity:** Ensuring data accuracy and reliability at scale.

---

2. Introduction to Dask

Dask is a Python library designed for parallel computing, allowing you to process data larger than memory by breaking it into manageable chunks.

Key Features:

- Works seamlessly with familiar libraries like Pandas and NumPy.
- Scales computations from a single machine to distributed clusters.
- Supports dataframes, arrays, and machine learning workflows.

Installing Dask

bash

```
pip install dask
```

Getting Started with Dask

- **Creating a Dask DataFrame:**

python

```
import dask.dataframe as dd

# Load a large CSV file into a Dask DataFrame
df = dd.read_csv("large_dataset.csv")
print(df.head())  # Preview the first few rows
```

- **Lazy**   **Evaluation:**

Unlike Pandas, Dask doesn't compute results immediately. Instead, it builds a computation graph and executes it only when required.

python

```python
# Perform operations
mean_value = df["column"].mean()

# Trigger computation
print(mean_value.compute())
```

3. Handling Big Data Efficiently

Chunking Large Files

Split large files into smaller chunks to avoid memory overload:

python

```python
df = dd.read_csv("large_dataset.csv", blocksize=25e6)  # 25MB chunks
```

Parallel Processing

Dask automatically parallelizes operations:

python

```python
df = dd.read_csv("large_dataset.csv")
result = df.groupby("category")["value"].sum().compute()
```

print(result)

Data Cleaning at Scale

Perform cleaning tasks on large datasets efficiently:

python

```
# Drop missing values
df_cleaned = df.dropna()

# Replace missing values
df_filled = df.fillna(0)
```

---

4. Comparing Dask to Pandas

Feature	Pandas	Dask
Dataset Size	Limited by RAM	Scales beyond RAM
Execution Mode	Eager	Lazy
Parallel Processing	No	Yes
Integration with Big Data	Limited	High

---

5. Use Case: Processing Large Datasets

Scenario: Analyzing a 10GB log file to identify trends and anomalies.

Step 1: Load the Data

python

```
import dask.dataframe as dd

# Load the log file
log_data = dd.read_csv("server_logs.csv")
print(log_data.head())
```

Step 2: Data Cleaning

python

```
# Handle missing values
log_data = log_data.dropna()

# Filter for relevant rows
filtered_logs = log_data[log_data["status_code"] == 200]
```

Step 3: Aggregation

python

```
# Group by date and count status codes
daily_counts = filtered_logs.groupby("date")["status_code"].count().compute()
print(daily_counts)
```

Step 4: Visualization

python

41

```
import matplotlib.pyplot as plt

# Plot the daily counts
daily_counts.plot(kind="bar")
plt.title("Daily Successful Requests")
plt.xlabel("Date")
plt.ylabel("Count")
plt.show()
```

---

6. Scaling Beyond a Single Machine

Using Dask Clusters

For extremely large datasets, you can distribute computations across multiple machines:

bash

```
dask-scheduler
dask-worker <scheduler-ip:port>
```

Integrating with Cloud Services

- AWS S3: Use Dask to process data stored in cloud buckets.

  python

  ```
  df = dd.read_csv("s3://bucket_name/large_dataset.csv")
  ```

- Google Cloud Storage and Azure Blob Storage are also supported.

---

7. Additional Tools for Big Data in Python

a. PySpark

- Apache Spark's Python API for distributed data processing.
- Works well for big data pipelines and ETL (Extract, Transform, Load) tasks.

b. Vaex

- Similar to Dask but optimized for in-memory, out-of-core processing.
- Faster for some exploratory data analysis tasks.

c. RAPIDS

- NVIDIA's GPU-accelerated library for big data processing.

---

8. Practical Example: Combining Pandas and Dask

Handle datasets that are too large for Pandas but benefit from both libraries:

python

```python
import pandas as pd
import dask.dataframe as dd

# Use Dask for initial processing
df_dask = dd.read_csv("large_dataset.csv")
df_cleaned = df_dask.dropna().compute()

# Use Pandas for final analysis
df_pandas = pd.DataFrame(df_cleaned)
summary = df_pandas.describe()
print(summary)
```

By leveraging Dask and other Python tools, you can handle large datasets efficiently and scale your workflows to meet the demands of real-world big data challenges. This chapter has equipped you with the foundational knowledge to process, analyze, and visualize big data, preparing you for advanced AI and data science tasks.

Chapter 4: Setting Up Your AI Workspace

Overview

A well-configured workspace is essential for efficient AI and data science workflows. This chapter guides you through setting up Python environments, choosing the right Integrated Development Environment (IDE), and installing the tools and libraries needed to kickstart your journey into AI and data science.

---

1. Setting Up Python Environments

Why Use Virtual Environments?

- Isolate projects to avoid dependency conflicts.
- Ensure reproducibility by maintaining specific library versions.
- Keep your global Python installation clean.

Creating and Managing Virtual Environments

1. **Using**   **venv:**

   A lightweight virtual environment built into Python.

   bash

```
python -m venv ai_workspace
source ai_workspace/bin/activate  # On Linux/Mac
ai_workspace\Scripts\activate    # On Windows
```

2. **Using** **conda:**

Ideal for data science due to easy package management.

bash

```
conda create -n ai_workspace python=3.10
conda activate ai_workspace
```

3. **Managing Dependencies:** Create a requirements.txt file to save dependencies:

bash

```
pip freeze > requirements.txt
```
Install dependencies:

bash

```
pip install -r requirements.txt
```

---

2. Choosing an IDE or Code Editor

Popular Options for AI and Data Science

- **Jupyter Notebook:**
    - Best for exploratory data analysis and visualizations.
    - Supports Markdown and inline visualizations.
    - Installation:

    bash

    pip install notebook

    - Launch:

    bash

    jupyter notebook

- **VS Code:**
    - Lightweight with extensive extensions.
    - Key Extensions:
        - Python
        - Jupyter
        - Pylance (for intelligent autocompletion)
    - Configuration:

    bash

    pip install pylint

- **PyCharm:**

- o Comprehensive IDE with advanced debugging and refactoring tools.
- o Community edition is free for most users.
- **Google Colab:**
  - o Free cloud-based Jupyter Notebook.
  - o No setup required; provides free GPU resources.
  - o Access it at Google Colab.

Recommendation:

Use Jupyter Notebook for exploration and visualization and VS Code for structured development.

---

3. Installing Essential Libraries and Tools

Core Libraries for AI and Data Science

1. **Data Manipulation:**
   - o Pandas, NumPy
   - o Installation:

     bash

     pip install pandas numpy

2. **Data Visualization:**
   - o Matplotlib, Seaborn

- o Installation:

  bash

  pip install matplotlib seaborn

3. **Machine Learning:**
   - o Scikit-learn
   - o Installation:

     bash

     pip install scikit-learn

4. **Deep Learning:**
   - o TensorFlow, PyTorch
   - o Installation:

     bash

     pip install tensorflow
     pip install torch torchvision

5. **Big Data Processing:**
   - o Dask, PySpark
   - o Installation:

     bash

     pip install dask pyspark

Version Control with Git

- Track and manage changes in your projects.
- Installation:
  - ○ Windows: Install via Git for Windows.
  - ○ Linux/Mac: Use the package manager (apt, brew, etc.).
- Basic Commands:

bash

```
git init
git add .
git commit -m "Initial commit"
git push origin main
```

---

4. Configuring Your Workspace for Efficiency

Organizing Your Projects

1. **Directory Structure:**
   - ○ Follow a clear, consistent directory structure:

kotlin

```
ai_project/
├── data/
├── notebooks/
├── scripts/
```

```
├── models/
└── requirements.txt
```

2. **README Files:**

   o Include a README.md in each project directory to document its purpose and usage.

Setting Environment Variables

- Store sensitive information like API keys securely.

  bash

  export API_KEY="your_api_key"

Automating Tasks with Makefiles

- Simplify common tasks like testing and deploying.

  makefile

  run:
      python main.py

---

5. Optimizing for Large-Scale AI Projects

Using Docker for Containerization

- Package your AI environment and dependencies into a container for reproducibility.
- Installation:
    o Download Docker.
- Basic Dockerfile:

dockerfile

```
FROM python:3.10
WORKDIR /app
COPY requirements.txt .
RUN pip install -r requirements.txt
CMD ["python", "main.py"]
```

Distributed Computing Tools

- **Dask or Apache Airflow:** Automate and scale data pipelines.
- **Kubernetes:** Manage and deploy AI applications in clusters.

---

6. Testing and Debugging Tools

Debugging with Python's pdb

- Debug code interactively.

python

```
import pdb
pdb.set_trace()
```

Automated Testing with Pytest

- Write unit tests to ensure code quality.

bash

```
pip install pytest
```

Example Test File:

python

```
def test_addition():
    assert 1 + 1 == 2
```

Linting and Code Style

- Use pylint and black to maintain clean code.

bash

```
pip install pylint black
pylint your_script.py
black your_script.py
```

---

7. Practical Example: Your First AI Workspace Setup

Here's a complete script to set up an AI workspace:

bash

```bash
# Create a virtual environment
python -m venv ai_workspace
source ai_workspace/bin/activate

# Install essential libraries
pip install pandas numpy matplotlib seaborn scikit-learn tensorflow

# Initialize Git repository
git init
echo "venv/" >> .gitignore

# Create project structure
mkdir -p ai_project/{data,notebooks,scripts,models}
touch ai_project/README.md
```

This chapter has provided a comprehensive guide to setting up your AI workspace. By configuring Python environments, choosing the right tools, and organizing your projects, you'll create a productive environment that supports both small-scale exploration and large-scale AI deployments. With this setup, you're ready to tackle data science and AI challenges efficiently.

Chapter 5: Version Control with Git

Overview

Version control is critical for managing AI projects, ensuring collaboration, tracking changes, and maintaining reproducibility. Git is the most widely used version control system, and pairing it with GitHub (or similar platforms) provides a powerful workflow for collaborative development.

---

1. Why Use Version Control for AI Projects?

- **Collaboration:** Enable teams to work on the same project without overwriting each other's work.
- **Tracking Changes:** Keep a detailed history of code modifications and revert to previous versions if necessary.
- **Reproducibility:** Facilitate clean tracking of model versions, data updates, and experimental setups.
- **Backup and Security:** Store code safely in remote repositories like GitHub, GitLab, or Bitbucket.

---

2. Installing and Setting Up Git

Installation

1. **Windows:** Download and install Git from git-scm.com.

2. **Linux:** Install using your package manager:

   bash

   ```
   sudo apt-get install git  # Debian/Ubuntu
   sudo yum install git      # CentOS/RedHat
   ```

3. **macOS:** Install via Homebrew:

   bash

   ```
   brew install git
   ```

Configuration

Set up your username and email:

bash

```
git config --global user.name "Your Name"
git config --global user.email "your.email@example.com"
```

View the configuration:

bash

```
git config --list
```

---

3. Basic Git Commands

Initializing a Repository

- Create a Git repository in your project directory:

bash

git init

Adding and Committing Changes

1. Add files to the staging area:

bash

git add <file_name>
git add . # Add all changes

2. Commit changes:

bash

git commit -m "Initial commit"

Viewing the Status

- Check the status of your repository:

bash

git status

Viewing Commit History

- See the log of all commits:

bash

git log

---

4. Collaborating with GitHub

Setting Up a Repository on GitHub

1. Create a new repository on GitHub.
2. Link the local repository to the GitHub repository:

bash

git remote add origin https://github.com/yourusername/your-repo.git

Pushing Changes to GitHub

1. Push your changes to the remote repository:

bash

git push -u origin main

2. For subsequent pushes:

bash

git push

Cloning a Repository

- Clone an existing repository:

bash

git clone https://github.com/yourusername/your-repo.git

---

5. Branching and Merging

Creating and Switching Branches

- Create a new branch:

bash

git branch feature-branch

- Switch to the branch:

bash

git checkout feature-branch

- Create and switch in one step:

bash

git checkout -b feature-branch

Merging Branches

- Merge a branch into the main branch:

bash

```
git checkout main
git merge feature-branch
```

6. Handling Conflicts

Conflicts occur when multiple contributors modify the same lines of code. Resolve conflicts by editing the conflicting files and marking resolved sections.

1. Identify conflicts:

bash

```
git status
```

2. Resolve conflicts in your editor.
3. Add and commit the resolved file:

bash

```
git add <file_name>
git commit
```

7. Advanced Git Features

Stashing Changes

- Temporarily save changes without committing:

  bash

  git stash

- Apply stashed changes:

  bash

  git stash apply

Reverting Commits

- Undo the last commit without losing changes:

  bash

  git reset --soft HEAD~1

- Undo a commit completely:

  bash

  git reset --hard HEAD~1

Tagging

- Tag a specific commit (e.g., for a version release):

bash

git tag -a v1.0 -m "Version 1.0"

---

8. Workflow for AI Projects

Managing Code and Data

- **Track Code, Not Data:** Use .gitignore to exclude large datasets or model files from version control. Example .gitignore file:

  bash

  data/
  models/
  *.log

Experiment Tracking

- Create separate branches for experiments:

  bash

  git checkout -b experiment-branch

- Merge only successful experiments into the main branch.

---

9. Practical Example: Collaborative AI Project

Scenario: Building a Machine Learning Model

1. Initialize a repository:

   bash

   ```
   git init
   ```

2. Add and commit files:

   bash

   ```
   git add data_preprocessing.py
   git commit -m "Added data preprocessing script"
   ```

3. Push changes to GitHub:

   bash

   ```
   git push origin main
   ```

4. Create a branch for a new model:

   bash

   ```
   git checkout -b model-training
   ```

5. Merge the branch after testing:

```bash
git checkout main
git merge model-training
```

---

10. Integration with AI Tools

Using Git with Jupyter Notebooks

- Track notebook changes with Git extensions like nbdime:

```bash
pip install nbdime
nbdime config-git --enable
```

GitHub Actions for Automation

- Automate tasks like testing and deployment using GitHub Actions.
- Example workflow (.github/workflows/main.yml):

```yaml
name: CI Pipeline

on: [push]

jobs:
```

```
test:
  runs-on: ubuntu-latest
  steps:
  - uses: actions/checkout@v2
  - name: Set up Python
    uses: actions/setup-python@v2
    with:
      python-version: '3.9'
  - name: Install dependencies
    run: pip install -r requirements.txt
  - name: Run tests
    run: pytest
```

Git and GitHub provide a robust foundation for managing AI projects, enabling seamless collaboration, version tracking, and reproducibility. Mastering Git will empower you to handle complex workflows and ensure your AI projects remain organized and efficient.

Chapter 6: Data Cleaning and Preprocessing

Overview

Data cleaning and preprocessing are critical steps in any data science workflow. Clean, well-prepared data improves model accuracy, reduces bias, and ensures meaningful insights. This chapter covers essential techniques like handling missing data, scaling, and encoding, with practical examples using Python libraries like **Pandas** and **Scikit-learn**.

---

1. The Importance of Data Cleaning

- **Garbage In, Garbage Out:** Poor-quality data leads to inaccurate models and unreliable insights.

- **Improving Model Performance:** Preprocessed data reduces noise, ensures feature uniformity, and enhances model predictions.

- **Ensuring Interpretability:** Clean data is easier to visualize, understand, and communicate.

---

2. Handling Missing Data

Causes of Missing Data

- Human error in data entry.
- Equipment malfunctions during data collection.
- Intentional omission of sensitive information.

Identifying Missing Data

- **Using Pandas:**

  python

  ```python
  import pandas as pd

  # Load dataset
  data = pd.DataFrame({
      "Name": ["Alice", "Bob", "Charlie", None],
      "Age": [25, None, 30, 22],
      "Salary": [50000, 60000, None, 45000]
  })

  # Check for missing values
  print(data.isnull())
  print(data.isnull().sum())
  ```

Techniques to Handle Missing Data

1. **Removing Missing Data:**
   - Drop rows or columns with missing values.

python

```python
data.dropna(inplace=True)  # Drop rows
data.dropna(axis=1, inplace=True)  # Drop columns
```

2. Imputing Missing Values:

- o Replace missing values with statistical metrics like mean, median, or mode.

python

```python
data['Age'].fillna(data['Age'].mean(), inplace=True)  # Mean
data['Salary'].fillna(data['Salary'].median(), inplace=True)  # Median
```

- o Use Scikit-learn's SimpleImputer for more control:

python

```python
from sklearn.impute import SimpleImputer

imputer = SimpleImputer(strategy="mean")
data['Age'] = imputer.fit_transform(data[['Age']])
```

3. Advanced Imputation Techniques:

- o Use predictive models to fill in missing data (e.g., K-Nearest Neighbors).

python

```python
from sklearn.impute import KNNImputer
```

```
knn_imputer = KNNImputer(n_neighbors=2)
data_imputed = knn_imputer.fit_transform(data)
```

---

3. Scaling and Normalization

Why Scale Data?

- Features with varying scales (e.g., income vs. age) can bias machine learning models.
- Scaling ensures all features contribute equally to the model.

Techniques for Scaling

1. **Standardization:**
   - Centers data around the mean with unit variance.

   python

   ```
   from sklearn.preprocessing import StandardScaler

   scaler = StandardScaler()
   data_scaled = scaler.fit_transform(data[['Age', 'Salary']])
   ```

2. **Normalization:**
   - Scales data to a range between 0 and 1.

   python

```
from sklearn.preprocessing import MinMaxScaler

normalizer = MinMaxScaler()
data_normalized = normalizer.fit_transform(data[['Age', 'Salary']])
```

3. **Robust Scaling:**

   o Reduces the influence of outliers.

python

```
from sklearn.preprocessing import RobustScaler

robust_scaler = RobustScaler()
data_robust = robust_scaler.fit_transform(data[['Age', 'Salary']])
```

---

4. Encoding Categorical Variables

Why Encode Categorical Data?

- Machine learning models cannot directly process non-numeric data.
- Encoding converts categorical features into numerical formats.

Techniques for Encoding

1. **Label Encoding:**

   o Assigns a unique integer to each category.

python

from sklearn.preprocessing import LabelEncoder

encoder = LabelEncoder()
data['Category'] = encoder.fit_transform(data['Category'])

2. One-Hot Encoding:

o   Converts categories into binary columns.

python

data = pd.get_dummies(data, columns=["Category"])

3. Ordinal Encoding:

o   For ordinal data with inherent order (e.g., low, medium, high).

python

from sklearn.preprocessing import OrdinalEncoder

ordinal_encoder = OrdinalEncoder(categories=[["low", "medium", "high"]])
data['Category'] = ordinal_encoder.fit_transform(data[['Category']])

5. Feature Transformation

Log Transformation:

- Reduces skewness in highly skewed data.

python

```
import numpy as np
data['Salary'] = np.log1p(data['Salary'])  # Log transform with protection for 0 values
```

Binning:

- Group continuous variables into discrete bins.

python

```
data['Age_Group'] = pd.cut(data['Age'], bins=[0, 18, 35, 60], labels=["Young", "Adult", "Senior"])
```

Polynomial Features:

- Create interaction terms for feature enhancement.

python

```
from sklearn.preprocessing import PolynomialFeatures

poly = PolynomialFeatures(degree=2)
data_poly = poly.fit_transform(data[['Age', 'Salary']])
```

6. Automating Data Cleaning

Using Pipelines:

- Combine multiple preprocessing steps into a pipeline.

python

```python
from sklearn.pipeline import Pipeline

pipeline = Pipeline([
    ('imputer', SimpleImputer(strategy="mean")),
    ('scaler', StandardScaler())
])

data_preprocessed = pipeline.fit_transform(data[['Age', 'Salary']])
```

Creating Reusable Functions:

- Automate repetitive tasks with Python functions.

python

```python
def clean_data(df):
    df.fillna(df.mean(), inplace=True)
    df = pd.get_dummies(df, drop_first=True)
    return df

data_cleaned = clean_data(data)
```

7. Practical Example: Data Cleaning Workflow

Scenario: Cleaning a Customer Dataset

python

```python
import pandas as pd
from sklearn.impute import SimpleImputer
from sklearn.preprocessing import StandardScaler, OneHotEncoder
from sklearn.compose import ColumnTransformer

# Load dataset
data = pd.DataFrame({
    "Name": ["Alice", "Bob", "Charlie", None],
    "Age": [25, None, 30, 22],
    "Salary": [50000, 60000, None, 45000],
    "Gender": ["Female", "Male", "Male", "Female"]
})

# Impute missing values
imputer = SimpleImputer(strategy="mean")
data['Age'] = imputer.fit_transform(data[['Age']])

# Scale numerical features
scaler = StandardScaler()
data[['Age', 'Salary']] = scaler.fit_transform(data[['Age', 'Salary']])

# Encode categorical features
encoder = OneHotEncoder()
gender_encoded = encoder.fit_transform(data[['Gender']]).toarray()
data[['Female', 'Male']] = gender_encoded

# Drop original categorical column
```

```
data.drop(columns=['Gender'], inplace=True)

print(data)
```

Data cleaning and preprocessing are indispensable steps in the data science pipeline. By mastering techniques for handling missing data, scaling, and encoding, you ensure that your datasets are ready for analysis and modeling. This chapter provides a foundation to process messy data into a reliable format, setting you up for success in subsequent analyses and machine learning workflows.

Chapter 7: Exploratory Data Analysis (EDA)

Overview

Exploratory Data Analysis (EDA) is the process of visualizing and analyzing datasets to uncover patterns, relationships, and anomalies. It serves as a foundation for building effective models by offering deep insights into the data. In this chapter, you'll learn how to perform EDA using Python libraries like **Pandas**, **Matplotlib**, and **Seaborn**.

---

1. Importance of EDA

- **Understanding Data Distribution:** Identify patterns, trends, and outliers.

- **Feature Selection:** Discover the most relevant features for modeling.

- **Detecting Data Issues:** Spot missing data, duplicates, and incorrect values.

- **Hypothesis Generation:** Formulate questions and hypotheses about the data.

---

2. Steps in EDA

Step 1: Load and Inspect the Data

- Use Pandas to load and explore datasets:

python

```
import pandas as pd

# Load dataset
data = pd.read_csv("data.csv")

# View basic information
print(data.head())     # First 5 rows
print(data.info())     # Data types and non-null counts
print(data.describe()) # Summary statistics
```

Step 2: Check for Missing Values

- Identify missing data:

python

```
print(data.isnull().sum())
```

- Visualize missing data with Seaborn:

python

```
import seaborn as sns
```

```
import matplotlib.pyplot as plt
```

```
sns.heatmap(data.isnull(), cbar=False, cmap="viridis")
plt.title("Missing Data Heatmap")
plt.show()
```

Step 3: Check for Duplicates

- Remove duplicates:

```python
python
```

```
data = data.drop_duplicates()
```

---

3. Univariate Analysis

Analyze individual variables to understand their distribution.

Categorical Variables

- Use bar plots for visualizing counts:

```python
python
```

```
sns.countplot(data=data, x="Category")
plt.title("Category Distribution")
plt.show()
```

Numerical Variables

- Visualize distributions with histograms and boxplots:

python

```
# Histogram
data["Age"].plot(kind="hist", bins=20, title="Age Distribution")

# Boxplot
sns.boxplot(data=data, x="Age")
plt.title("Age Boxplot")
plt.show()
```

4. Bivariate Analysis

Examine relationships between two variables.

Numerical vs. Numerical

- Use scatter plots and correlation matrices:

python

```
# Scatter plot
sns.scatterplot(data=data, x="Age", y="Salary")
plt.title("Age vs. Salary")
plt.show()

# Correlation matrix
correlation = data.corr()
```

```
sns.heatmap(correlation, annot=True, cmap="coolwarm")
plt.title("Correlation Matrix")
plt.show()
```

Categorical vs. Numerical

- Use boxplots and bar plots:

  python

  ```
  # Boxplot
  sns.boxplot(data=data, x="Category", y="Salary")
  plt.title("Salary by Category")
  plt.show()
  ```

Categorical vs. Categorical

- Use stacked bar plots or cross-tabulations:

  python

  ```
  pd.crosstab(data["Category"],          data["Gender"]).plot(kind="bar",
  stacked=True)
  plt.title("Category by Gender")
  plt.show()
  ```

---

5. Multivariate Analysis

Examine relationships involving more than two variables.

Pairplot

Visualize relationships between all numerical variables:

python

```
sns.pairplot(data=data, hue="Category")
plt.show()
```

Heatmaps

Analyze correlations and patterns:

python

```
sns.heatmap(data.corr(), annot=True, cmap="coolwarm")
plt.title("Feature Correlation")
plt.show()
```

6. Outlier Detection

Identify and handle extreme values that could distort analysis.

Using Boxplots

python

```
sns.boxplot(data=data, x="Salary")
plt.title("Outlier Detection for Salary")
plt.show()
```

Using Z-Scores

python

```
from scipy.stats import zscore
```

```
data["Z_Score"] = zscore(data["Salary"])
outliers = data[data["Z_Score"].abs() > 3]
print(outliers)
```

Using the Interquartile Range (IQR)

python

```
Q1 = data["Salary"].quantile(0.25)
Q3 = data["Salary"].quantile(0.75)
IQR = Q3 - Q1
```

```
outliers = data[(data["Salary"] < Q1 - 1.5 * IQR) | (data["Salary"] > Q3 + 1.5 * IQR)]
print(outliers)
```

---

7. Feature Relationships and Insights

Example: Age and Salary

- Hypothesis: Older employees earn higher salaries.
- Analysis:

  python

  ```
  sns.scatterplot(data=data, x="Age", y="Salary")
  plt.title("Age vs. Salary")
  ```

```
plt.show()
```

Example: Gender and Salary

- Hypothesis: Gender impacts salary distribution.
- Analysis:

python

```
sns.boxplot(data=data, x="Gender", y="Salary")
plt.title("Salary Distribution by Gender")
plt.show()
```

---

8. Automating EDA

Using Pandas Profiling

Generate a detailed EDA report:

bash

```
pip install pandas-profiling
python
```

```
from pandas_profiling import ProfileReport
```

```
profile = ProfileReport(data)
profile.to_file("eda_report.html")
```

Using Sweetviz

Another library for automated EDA:

bash

```
pip install sweetviz
python

import sweetviz as sv

report = sv.analyze(data)
report.show_html("sweetviz_report.html")
```

---

9. Practical Example: EDA Workflow

Scenario: Analyzing a Customer Churn Dataset

```python
import pandas as pd
import seaborn as sns
import matplotlib.pyplot as plt

# Load dataset
data = pd.read_csv("customer_churn.csv")

# Missing data heatmap
sns.heatmap(data.isnull(), cbar=False, cmap="viridis")
plt.title("Missing Data Heatmap")
plt.show()

# Churn distribution
sns.countplot(data=data, x="Churn")
```

```
plt.title("Churn Distribution")
plt.show()

# Correlation heatmap
correlation = data.corr()
sns.heatmap(correlation, annot=True, cmap="coolwarm")
plt.title("Correlation Matrix")
plt.show()

# Pairplot
sns.pairplot(data=data, hue="Churn")
plt.show()
```

Exploratory Data Analysis is the bridge between raw data and actionable insights. By mastering the techniques of visualization and analysis, you can uncover patterns, detect anomalies, and prepare data effectively for modeling. This chapter equips you with the tools to make data-driven decisions confidently.

Chapter 8: Introduction to Statistics for AI

Overview

Statistics is the backbone of AI and data science. It provides the tools to analyze data, make inferences, and build predictive models. This chapter introduces core statistical concepts and demonstrates their application in AI workflows.

---

1. Importance of Statistics in AI

- **Data Analysis:** Understand data distributions, trends, and anomalies.
- **Inference:** Draw s and predictions based on sample data.
- **Model Evaluation:** Use statistical methods to validate AI models.
- **Decision-Making:** Support AI systems in making informed, data-driven decisions.

---

2. Types of Statistics

Descriptive Statistics

Summarizes data to provide insights into its structure and distribution.

- Examples: Mean, median, mode, standard deviation.

Inferential Statistics

Makes predictions or inferences about a population from a sample.

- Examples: Hypothesis testing, confidence intervals.

---

3. Key Statistical Concepts

Measures of Central Tendency

1. **Mean (Average):**
    - Sum of all values divided by the number of values.

    python

    ```
    import numpy as np
    data = [10, 20, 30, 40, 50]
    print(np.mean(data))  # Output: 30.0
    ```

2. **Median:**
    - The middle value in sorted data.

    python

```python
print(np.median(data)) # Output: 30.0
```

3. Mode:

- o The most frequently occurring value.

python

```python
from scipy import stats
print(stats.mode(data))    # Output: ModeResult(mode=array([10]),
count=array([1]))
```

Measures of Dispersion

1. Range:

- o Difference between the maximum and minimum values.

python

```python
print(max(data) - min(data)) # Output: 40
```

2. Variance:

- o Average of squared differences from the mean.

python

```python
print(np.var(data)) # Output: 200.0
```

3. Standard Deviation:

- o Square root of variance, indicating data spread.

python

print(np.std(data)) # Output: 14.14

---

4. Probability in AI

Probability is the foundation of machine learning, enabling models to predict outcomes based on uncertainty.

Basic Probability

- Probability of an event $P(A)P(A)P(A)$: P(A)=Number of favorable outcomesTotal number of outco mesP(A) = \frac{\text{Number of favorable outcomes}}{\text{Total number of outcomes}}P(A)=Total number of outcomesNumber of favorable outcomes

Conditional Probability

- Probability of AAA given BBB $(P(A|B)P(A|B)P(A|B))$: P(A|B)=P(A∩B)P(B)```P(A|B) = \frac{P(A \cap B)}{P(B)}```P(A|B)=P(B)P(A∩B)```

Bayes' Theorem

- Used in classification algorithms like Naive Bayes: $P(A|B)=P(B|A)\cdot P(A)P(B)P(A|B)$ = \frac{P(B|A) \cdot P(A)}{P(B)}$P(A|B)=P(B)P(B|A)\cdot P(A)$

Applications in AI

- Predicting class probabilities (e.g., spam detection).
- Estimating likelihoods in probabilistic models.

---

5. Hypothesis Testing

Hypothesis testing determines if there is enough evidence to support a claim.

Steps in Hypothesis Testing

1. **Null Hypothesis (H0H_0H0):** Default assumption (e.g., no difference in means).
2. **Alternative Hypothesis (HaH_aHa):** The claim to be tested (e.g., significant difference).
3. **Significance Level (α\alpha$\alpha$):** Threshold for rejecting H0H_0H0 (commonly 0.05).
4. **P-value:** Probability of observing results as extreme as those in the sample.
   - If P-value$<\alpha$\text{P-value} < \alpha$P-value$<\alpha$, reject H0H_0H0.

Example: T-Test

Test whether two sample means are significantly different:

python

```
from scipy.stats import ttest_ind

data1 = [10, 20, 30]
data2 = [15, 25, 35]
t_stat, p_value = ttest_ind(data1, data2)
print(f"T-Statistic: {t_stat}, P-Value: {p_value}")
```

---

6. Correlation and Regression

Correlation

Measures the strength and direction of a relationship between two variables.

- **Pearson Correlation Coefficient (rrr):**
  r=Covariance(X,Y)σX·σYr $= \frac{\text{Covariance}(X, Y)}{\sigma_X \cdot \sigma_Y}$r=σX·σYCovariance(X,Y)

  python

  ```
  import numpy as np
  data_x = [1, 2, 3, 4]
  data_y = [10, 20, 30, 40]
  print(np.corrcoef(data_x, data_y))  # Output: [[1. 1.][1. 1.]]
  ```

Linear Regression

Models the relationship between a dependent variable YYY and one or more independent variables XXX.

- Simple Linear Regression Equation: $Y=\beta_0+\beta_1X+\square Y =$ \beta_0 + \beta_1 X + \epsilon $Y=\beta_0+\beta_1X+\square$

python

```
from sklearn.linear_model import LinearRegression
import numpy as np

X = np.array([1, 2, 3, 4]).reshape(-1, 1)
y = np.array([10, 20, 30, 40])
model = LinearRegression()
model.fit(X, y)
print(f"Coefficient: {model.coef_}, Intercept: {model.intercept_}")
```

7. Advanced Topics

Chi-Square Test

Used for categorical data to test independence between variables:

python

```
from scipy.stats import chi2_contingency

data = [[10, 20], [20, 30]]
chi2, p, dof, expected = chi2_contingency(data)
```

```python
print(f"Chi2: {chi2}, P-value: {p}")
```

ANOVA (Analysis of Variance)

Tests differences among group means:

python

```python
from scipy.stats import f_oneway

group1 = [10, 20, 30]
group2 = [15, 25, 35]
group3 = [20, 30, 40]
f_stat, p_value = f_oneway(group1, group2, group3)
print(f"F-Statistic: {f_stat}, P-Value: {p_value}")
```

8. Practical Example: Statistical Insights for AI

Scenario: Employee Data Analysis

Analyze a dataset containing employee salaries and ages to identify relationships and test hypotheses.

python

```python
import pandas as pd
from scipy.stats import ttest_ind, pearsonr

# Sample data
data = pd.DataFrame({
    "Age": [25, 30, 35, 40, 45],
    "Salary": [50000, 60000, 70000, 80000, 90000]
```

```
})

# Descriptive statistics
print(data.describe())

# Correlation
corr, _ = pearsonr(data["Age"], data["Salary"])
print(f"Correlation: {corr}")

# T-test for salaries between two age groups
group1 = data[data["Age"] <= 35]["Salary"]
group2 = data[data["Age"] > 35]["Salary"]
t_stat, p_value = ttest_ind(group1, group2)
print(f"T-Statistic: {t_stat}, P-Value: {p_value}")
```

Statistics is indispensable for AI and data science, forming the foundation for data exploration, modeling, and validation. By understanding core statistical methods, you can interpret data more effectively and enhance your AI models with data-driven insights.

Chapter 9: Feature Engineering and Selection

Overview

Feature engineering and selection are critical steps in building effective AI models. Feature engineering involves creating new, meaningful features from raw data, while feature selection identifies the most relevant features for a model, improving accuracy and reducing complexity.

1. Importance of Feature Engineering and Selection

Feature Engineering:

- Enhances predictive power by creating new features that better capture patterns.
- Transforms raw data into formats suitable for machine learning.

Feature Selection:

- Reduces overfitting by eliminating irrelevant or redundant features.
- Improves computational efficiency by reducing dataset dimensionality.

2. Feature Engineering Techniques

1. Handling Missing Values

- Fill missing values with domain-specific knowledge, statistical methods, or predictions.

python

```
data['Age'] = data['Age'].fillna(data['Age'].mean())
```

2. Creating Derived Features

- Generate new features based on existing ones:
  - **Ratios:**

python

```
data['Income_to_Debt_Ratio'] = data['Income'] / data['Debt']
```

  - **Date-Based   Features:**
  Extract information like year, month, or day:

python

```
data['Year'] = pd.to_datetime(data['Date']).dt.year
```

      o **Text   Features:**

Analyze word or character counts in textual data:

python

```
data['Word_Count'] = data['Text_Column'].apply(lambda x: len(x.split()))
```

3. Scaling and Transformation

- **Log   Transformation:**
  For skewed data:

python

```
data['Log_Income'] = np.log1p(data['Income'])
```

- **Binning:**
  Group continuous variables into discrete bins:

python

```
data['Age_Group'] = pd.cut(data['Age'], bins=[0, 18, 35, 60], labels=['Child', 'Adult', 'Senior'])
```

4. Encoding Categorical Features

- **One-Hot Encoding:**

python

```
data = pd.get_dummies(data, columns=['Category'])
```

- **Ordinal Encoding:**

python

```
from sklearn.preprocessing import OrdinalEncoder
encoder = OrdinalEncoder(categories=[['low', 'medium', 'high']])
data['Category'] = encoder.fit_transform(data[['Category']])
```

---

3. Feature Selection Techniques

1. Filter Methods

Select features based on statistical properties of the data.

- **Correlation Matrix:** Identify highly correlated features:

python

```
import seaborn as sns
correlation = data.corr()
sns.heatmap(correlation, annot=True)
```

- **Chi-Square Test:** For categorical data:

python

```
from sklearn.feature_selection import chi2
chi_scores = chi2(X, y)
```

2. Wrapper Methods

Evaluate subsets of features by training models.

- **Recursive Feature Elimination (RFE):** Iteratively removes features and evaluates model performance:

python

```
from sklearn.feature_selection import RFE
from sklearn.linear_model import LogisticRegression

model = LogisticRegression()
rfe = RFE(model, n_features_to_select=5)
X_selected = rfe.fit_transform(X, y)
```

3. Embedded Methods

Integrate feature selection as part of the model training process.

- **Lasso Regularization:** Penalizes irrelevant features:

python

```
from sklearn.linear_model import Lasso

model = Lasso(alpha=0.1)
model.fit(X, y)
print(model.coef_)
```

- **Tree-Based Feature Importance:** Use tree models to rank feature importance:

```
python

from sklearn.ensemble import RandomForestClassifier

model = RandomForestClassifier()
model.fit(X, y)
print(model.feature_importances_)
```

---

4. Automating Feature Selection

Using Scikit-learn Pipelines

Combine preprocessing and feature selection in a pipeline:

```
python

from sklearn.pipeline import Pipeline
from sklearn.feature_selection import SelectKBest, f_classif
from sklearn.preprocessing import StandardScaler

pipeline = Pipeline([
    ('scaler', StandardScaler()),
    ('feature_selection', SelectKBest(score_func=f_classif, k=5)),
    ('model', LogisticRegression())
])

pipeline.fit(X, y)
```

Using Boruta for Feature Selection

Boruta is a powerful feature selection algorithm that identifies relevant features:

bash

```
pip install boruta
python

from boruta import BorutaPy
from sklearn.ensemble import RandomForestClassifier

model = RandomForestClassifier()
boruta_selector = BorutaPy(model, n_estimators='auto', random_state=42)
boruta_selector.fit(X.values, y.values)
```

5. Practical Example: Feature Engineering and Selection Workflow

Scenario: Predicting Customer Churn

You're tasked with improving a customer churn model by engineering meaningful features and selecting the most relevant ones.

Step 1: Load Data

python

```
import pandas as pd
data = pd.read_csv("customer_churn.csv")
```

Step 2: Engineer Features

python

```python
# Create income-to-debt ratio
data['Income_to_Debt'] = data['MonthlyIncome'] / data['TotalDebt']

# Extract year from contract start date
data['Contract_Year'] = pd.to_datetime(data['ContractStartDate']).dt.year
```

Step 3: Select Features

python

```python
from sklearn.feature_selection import SelectKBest, f_classif
X = data.drop(columns=['Churn'])
y = data['Churn']

selector = SelectKBest(score_func=f_classif, k=5)
X_selected = selector.fit_transform(X, y)
```

Step 4: Train Model with Selected Features

python

```python
from sklearn.ensemble import RandomForestClassifier
from sklearn.model_selection import train_test_split

X_train, X_test, y_train, y_test = train_test_split(X_selected, y, test_size=0.3, random_state=42)
model = RandomForestClassifier()
model.fit(X_train, y_train)
```

6. Best Practices

1. **Domain Knowledge:** Use domain expertise to guide feature engineering.
2. **Avoid Over-Engineering:** Keep features simple to prevent overfitting.
3. **Monitor Feature Importance:** Continuously evaluate feature contributions to model performance.

Feature engineering and selection are indispensable for building robust and efficient AI models. By transforming raw data into meaningful features and selecting the most relevant ones, you can significantly enhance model performance and reduce computational complexity. This chapter equips you with the techniques to make these processes effective and efficient.

Chapter 10: Working with Time-Series Data

Overview

Time-series data is sequential data recorded at specific time intervals (e.g., stock prices, weather data, or website traffic). Analyzing and forecasting time-series data is a critical skill in data science and AI. This chapter covers techniques to prepare, analyze, and model time-series data in Python.

---

1. Understanding Time-Series Data

Key Characteristics:

- **Trend:** Long-term increase or decrease in data.
- **Seasonality:** Regular patterns repeating over fixed intervals (e.g., daily, monthly).
- **Cyclic Patterns:** Fluctuations without fixed frequency, often driven by economic conditions.
- **Noise:** Random variations in the data.

Applications of Time-Series Analysis:

- Forecasting (e.g., sales, stock prices).
- Anomaly detection (e.g., fraud detection).

- Pattern recognition (e.g., energy usage).

---

2. Loading and Inspecting Time-Series Data

Loading Data:

python

```
import pandas as pd

# Load time-series dataset
data = pd.read_csv("time_series_data.csv", parse_dates=["Date"],
index_col="Date")
print(data.head())
```

Inspecting Data:

- View dataset summary:

  python

  ```
  print(data.info())
  print(data.describe())
  ```

- Plot time-series data:

  python

  ```
  import matplotlib.pyplot as plt
  ```

```
data["Value"].plot(figsize=(10, 5))
plt.title("Time-Series Data")
plt.xlabel("Date")
plt.ylabel("Value")
plt.show()
```

---

3. Preprocessing Time-Series Data

1. Handling Missing Values:

- Fill missing values:

python

```
data["Value"].fillna(method="ffill", inplace=True)  # Forward fill
```

2. Resampling Data:

- Aggregate data to different frequencies:

python

```
# Resample to monthly frequency
monthly_data = data["Value"].resample("M").mean()
print(monthly_data.head())
```

3. Detrending Data:

- Remove trends to focus on seasonality or cycles:

python

```
detrended = data["Value"] - data["Value"].rolling(window=12).mean()
```

4. Feature Engineering:

- Extract time-based features:

python

```
data["Year"] = data.index.year
data["Month"] = data.index.month
data["Day"] = data.index.day
data["DayOfWeek"] = data.index.dayofweek
```

4. Analyzing Time-Series Data

Decomposition:

- Decompose a time series into trend, seasonal, and residual components:

python

```
from statsmodels.tsa.seasonal import seasonal_decompose

decomposition          =          seasonal_decompose(data["Value"],
model="additive", period=12)
decomposition.plot()
```

```
plt.show()
```

Autocorrelation and Partial Autocorrelation:

- Visualize how data points are related to past values:

python

```
from statsmodels.graphics.tsaplots import plot_acf, plot_pacf

plot_acf(data["Value"])
plot_pacf(data["Value"])
plt.show()
```

---

5. Forecasting with Time-Series Data

1. Train-Test Split:
Ensure chronological order in splitting data:

python

```
split_point = int(len(data) * 0.8)
train, test = data[:split_point], data[split_point:]
```

2. Moving Average:

- Smooth data to identify trends:

python

```python
data["Moving_Avg"] = data["Value"].rolling(window=3).mean()
```

3. ARIMA Model:

A popular model combining **AutoRegression (AR)**, **Integration (I)**, and **Moving Average (MA)**:

python

```python
from statsmodels.tsa.arima.model import ARIMA

model = ARIMA(train["Value"], order=(1, 1, 1))
model_fit = model.fit()
print(model_fit.summary())

# Forecast
forecast = model_fit.forecast(steps=len(test))
```

4. Seasonal Decomposition of Time Series (SARIMA):

- Extend ARIMA to account for seasonality.

python

```python
from statsmodels.tsa.statespace.sarimax import SARIMAX

sarima_model = SARIMAX(train["Value"], order=(1, 1, 1), seasonal_order=(1, 1, 1, 12))
sarima_fit = sarima_model.fit()
forecast = sarima_fit.forecast(steps=len(test))
```

5. Exponential Smoothing:

- Handle both trends and seasonality.

python

```
from statsmodels.tsa.holtwinters import ExponentialSmoothing

model = ExponentialSmoothing(train["Value"], seasonal="add", seasonal_periods=12)
fit = model.fit()
forecast = fit.forecast(steps=len(test))
```

---

6. Advanced Techniques

LSTM for Time-Series Data:

Leverage deep learning for complex time-series patterns.

python

```
import numpy as np
from tensorflow.keras.models import Sequential
from tensorflow.keras.layers import LSTM, Dense

# Prepare data
X_train, y_train = [], []
for i in range(10, len(train)):
    X_train.append(train["Value"].values[i-10:i])
    y_train.append(train["Value"].values[i])
X_train, y_train = np.array(X_train), np.array(y_train)
```

```
# Build model
model = Sequential([
    LSTM(50, activation="relu", input_shape=(X_train.shape[1], 1)),
    Dense(1)
])
model.compile(optimizer="adam", loss="mse")
model.fit(X_train, y_train, epochs=20, batch_size=32)
```

7. Evaluating Model Performance

Metrics for Time-Series Models:

- ### Mean Absolute Error (MAE):

  python

  ```
  from sklearn.metrics import mean_absolute_error
  mae = mean_absolute_error(test["Value"], forecast)
  print(f'MAE: {mae}")
  ```

- ### Mean Squared Error (MSE):

  python

  ```
  from sklearn.metrics import mean_squared_error
  mse = mean_squared_error(test["Value"], forecast)
  print(f'MSE: {mse}")
  ```

- ### Mean Absolute Percentage Error (MAPE):

python

```
mape = np.mean(np.abs((test["Value"] - forecast) / test["Value"])) * 100
print(f"MAPE: {mape}%")
```

---

8. Practical Example: Forecasting Website Traffic

Scenario:

Predict website traffic for the next 30 days using historical data.

Step 1: Load and Visualize Data

python

```
data = pd.read_csv("website_traffic.csv", parse_dates=["Date"],
index_col="Date")
data["Traffic"].plot()
```

Step 2: Decompose Data

python

```
from statsmodels.tsa.seasonal import seasonal_decompose

seasonal_decompose(data["Traffic"], model="multiplicative").plot()
```

Step 3: Build ARIMA Model

python

```
from statsmodels.tsa.arima.model import ARIMA

model = ARIMA(data["Traffic"], order=(1, 1, 1))
```

```
model_fit = model.fit()
forecast = model_fit.forecast(steps=30)
print(forecast)
```

Step 4: Plot Forecast

python

```
plt.figure(figsize=(10, 5))
plt.plot(data["Traffic"], label="Actual")
plt.plot(forecast, label="Forecast", color="red")
plt.legend()
plt.show()
```

Time-series analysis is a crucial aspect of AI and data science, enabling predictions and insights from sequential data. This chapter equips you with the tools to preprocess, analyze, and forecast time-series data using Python, preparing you for real-world applications like financial forecasting, anomaly detection, and demand planning.

Chapter 11: Supervised Learning Fundamentals

Overview

Supervised learning is a core technique in machine learning where models are trained using labeled data to make predictions. This chapter explores the fundamentals of supervised learning with a focus on **linear regression** and **logistic regression**, along with key evaluation metrics.

---

1. Introduction to Supervised Learning

Supervised learning uses input-output pairs to train a model that maps inputs to outputs. It is divided into:

- **Regression:** Predicting continuous values (e.g., house prices).
- **Classification:** Predicting discrete categories (e.g., spam detection).

---

2. Linear Regression

Linear regression models the relationship between input variables XXX and a continuous output YYY:

$Y=\beta_0+\beta_1 X+\square$ $Y = \beta\_0 + \beta\_1 X + \epsilon Y = \beta_0+\beta_1 X+\square$

Where:

- β_0\beta_0β_0 is the intercept.
- β_1\beta_1β_1 is the slope.
- $\square$\epsilon$\square$ represents the error term.

Steps to Implement Linear Regression

1. Import Libraries

python

```
import numpy as np
import pandas as pd
from sklearn.model_selection import train_test_split
from sklearn.linear_model import LinearRegression
from sklearn.metrics import mean_squared_error, r2_score
```

2. Prepare Data

python

```
# Example dataset
data = pd.DataFrame({
    "Experience": [1, 2, 3, 4, 5],
    "Salary": [30000, 35000, 40000, 45000, 50000]
})
```

```
X = data[["Experience"]]
y = data["Salary"]
```

```
# Train-test split
X_train, X_test, y_train, y_test = train_test_split(X, y, test_size=0.2,
random_state=42)
```

3. Train the Model

python

```
model = LinearRegression()
model.fit(X_train, y_train)
```

```
# Coefficients
print(f"Intercept: {model.intercept_}")
print(f"Coefficient: {model.coef_}")
```

4. Make Predictions

python

```
y_pred = model.predict(X_test)
print(f"Predictions: {y_pred}")
```

5. Evaluate the Model

- **Mean Squared Error (MSE):**

$$MSE = \frac{1}{n} \sum_{i=1}^{n} (y_i - \hat{y}_i)^2$$

python

```
mse = mean_squared_error(y_test, y_pred)
print(f"MSE: {mse}")
```

- **R-Squared ($R2R^2R2$):** Measures how well the model explains the variability in the data.

$R2=1-SSresSStotR^2 \qquad = \qquad 1 \qquad -$
\frac{\text{SS}_{\text{res}}}{\text{SS}_{\text{tot}}}R2= 1-SStotSSres

python

```
r2 = r2_score(y_test, y_pred)
print(f"R^2 Score: {r2}")
```

---

3. Logistic Regression

Logistic regression is used for binary classification problems. It predicts probabilities and maps them to binary outcomes using the sigmoid function:

$P(y=1|X)=11+e-(\beta0+\beta1X)P(y=1|X) = \frac{1}{1 + e^{-(\beta_0 + \beta_1X)}}P(y=1|X)=1+e-(\beta0+\beta1X)1$

Steps to Implement Logistic Regression

1. Import Libraries

python

```
from sklearn.linear_model import LogisticRegression
from sklearn.metrics import accuracy_score, confusion_matrix, classification_report
```

2. Prepare Data

python

```
# Example dataset
data = pd.DataFrame({
    "Hours_Studied": [1, 2, 3, 4, 5],
    "Passed": [0, 0, 0, 1, 1]
})

X = data[["Hours_Studied"]]
y = data["Passed"]

# Train-test split
X_train, X_test, y_train, y_test = train_test_split(X, y, test_size=0.2, random_state=42)
```

3. Train the Model

python

```
model = LogisticRegression()
model.fit(X_train, y_train)
```

4. Make Predictions

python

```
y_pred = model.predict(X_test)
y_prob = model.predict_proba(X_test)[:, 1]
print(f"Predictions: {y_pred}")
print(f"Probabilities: {y_prob}")
```

5. Evaluate the Model

- **Accuracy:**

  $$\text{Accuracy} = \frac{\text{Correct Predictions}}{\text{Total Predictions}}$$

  python

  ```
  accuracy = accuracy_score(y_test, y_pred)
  print(f"Accuracy: {accuracy}")
  ```

- **Confusion Matrix:** Summarizes the performance of the model.

  python

  ```
  cm = confusion_matrix(y_test, y_pred)
  print(f"Confusion Matrix:\n{cm}")
  ```

- **Classification Report:** Provides precision, recall, and F1-score.

python

```
report = classification_report(y_test, y_pred)
print(report)
```

---

4. Comparing Linear and Logistic Regression

Feature	Linear Regression	Logistic Regression
Output Type	Continuous	Categorical (Binary/Multiclass)
Equation	$Y=\beta 0+\beta 1XY = \backslash beta\_0 + \backslash beta\_1XY=\beta 0+\beta 1X$	(P(y=1
Use Cases	Predicting prices, trends	Classifying spam emails, predicting churn

---

5. Practical Example: Predicting Student Pass/Fail

Dataset:

python

```
data = pd.DataFrame({
    "Study_Hours": [1, 2, 3, 4, 5, 6, 7, 8, 9, 10],
    "Pass": [0, 0, 0, 0, 1, 1, 1, 1, 1, 1]
})
```

```
X = data[["Study_Hours"]]
y = data["Pass"]


# Train-test split
X_train, X_test, y_train, y_test = train_test_split(X, y, test_size=0.2,
random_state=42)
```

Train and Evaluate Logistic Regression Model

python

```
model = LogisticRegression()
model.fit(X_train, y_train)


# Predictions
y_pred = model.predict(X_test)
y_prob = model.predict_proba(X_test)[:, 1]


# Evaluation
print(f"Accuracy: {accuracy_score(y_test, y_pred)}")
print(f"Confusion Matrix:\n{confusion_matrix(y_test, y_pred)}")
print(f"Classification Report:\n{classification_report(y_test, y_pred)}")
```

6. Best Practices

1. **Feature Scaling:** Standardize features for better performance.

2. **Cross-Validation:** Use cross-validation to ensure generalizability.

3. **Hyperparameter Tuning:** Optimize parameters using grid search or random search.

Linear and logistic regression are foundational supervised learning techniques. They provide insights into data relationships and form the basis for more advanced algorithms. By mastering these methods and their evaluation metrics, you can build robust regression and classification models for real-world applications.

Chapter 12: Tree-Based Models

Overview

Tree-based models are powerful and versatile algorithms used for both regression and classification. They include decision trees, random forests, and boosting techniques like XGBoost. These models handle non-linear relationships effectively and often achieve high predictive performance.

---

1. Decision Trees

What is a Decision Tree?

A decision tree is a flowchart-like model where each internal node represents a decision on a feature, each branch represents an outcome, and each leaf node represents a prediction.

Advantages:

- Easy to interpret and visualize.
- Handles both numerical and categorical data.
- Requires little data preprocessing.

Building a Decision Tree

1. **Import Libraries:**

python

```
from sklearn.tree import DecisionTreeClassifier, export_text, plot_tree
from sklearn.metrics import accuracy_score
```

2. Train a Decision Tree:

python

```
# Example dataset
data = {
    "Weather": ["Sunny", "Sunny", "Overcast", "Rain", "Rain"],
    "Play": [0, 0, 1, 1, 0]
}
df = pd.DataFrame(data)
X = pd.get_dummies(df[["Weather"]], drop_first=True)
y = df["Play"]

tree = DecisionTreeClassifier(max_depth=3, random_state=42)
tree.fit(X, y)
```

3. Visualize the Tree:

python

```
plot_tree(tree, feature_names=X.columns, class_names=["No", "Yes"],
filled=True)
```

4. Evaluate the Tree:

python

```
y_pred = tree.predict(X)
print(f"Accuracy: {accuracy_score(y, y_pred)}")
```

2. Random Forests

What is a Random Forest?

Random forests build multiple decision trees and combine their predictions to improve accuracy and reduce overfitting.

How it Works:

- **Bagging:** Each tree is trained on a random subset of the data.
- **Feature Subsampling:** Each tree considers only a random subset of features at each split.

Steps to Build a Random Forest

1. **Import Libraries:**

   python

   ```
   from sklearn.ensemble import RandomForestClassifier
   ```

2. **Train a Random Forest:**

   python

   ```
   rf = RandomForestClassifier(n_estimators=100, random_state=42)
   ```

```
rf.fit(X, y)
```

3. Feature Importance:

python

```python
import matplotlib.pyplot as plt

feature_importances = rf.feature_importances_
plt.barh(X.columns, feature_importances)
plt.title("Feature Importance")
plt.show()
```

4. Evaluate the Model:

python

```python
y_pred = rf.predict(X)
print(f"Accuracy: {accuracy_score(y, y_pred)}")
```

---

3. Boosting Techniques

What is Boosting?

Boosting combines multiple weak learners (e.g., shallow decision trees) in sequence, where each model corrects the errors of the previous one.

Types of Boosting:

- **AdaBoost:** Focuses on misclassified samples by assigning them higher weights.
- **Gradient Boosting:** Minimizes errors by optimizing a loss function.
- **XGBoost:** An advanced version of gradient boosting with improved speed and accuracy.

---

4. XGBoost

What is XGBoost?

XGBoost (Extreme Gradient Boosting) is a high-performance library for gradient boosting, known for its speed and accuracy.

Features:

- Regularization to prevent overfitting.
- Built-in handling of missing values.
- Parallelized tree construction.

Steps to Build an XGBoost Model

1. **Install XGBoost:**

bash

```
pip install xgboost
```

2. Train an XGBoost Model:

python

```python
from xgboost import XGBClassifier

xgb = XGBClassifier(n_estimators=100, learning_rate=0.1, max_depth=3, random_state=42)
xgb.fit(X, y)
```

3. Feature Importance:

python

```python
from xgboost import plot_importance

plot_importance(xgb)
plt.show()
```

4. Evaluate the Model:

python

```python
y_pred = xgb.predict(X)
print(f"Accuracy: {accuracy_score(y, y_pred)}")
```

---

5. Comparing Decision Trees, Random Forests, and XGBoost

Feature	Decision Tree	Random Forest	XGBoost
Interpretability	High	Moderate	Low
Overfitting Risk	High	Low	Very Low
Computational Efficiency	Low	Moderate	High
Performance	Moderate	High	Very High

6. Hyperparameter Tuning

Decision Tree:

- max_depth: Limits tree depth to prevent overfitting.
- min_samples_split: Minimum samples required to split a node.

Random Forest:

- n_estimators: Number of trees.
- max_features: Number of features to consider at each split.

XGBoost:

- learning_rate: Step size for each iteration.

- max_depth: Maximum depth of trees.
- n_estimators: Number of boosting rounds.

Using Grid Search for Optimization:

python

```
from sklearn.model_selection import GridSearchCV

param_grid = {
    'max_depth': [3, 5, 7],
    'n_estimators': [50, 100, 200]
}
grid = GridSearchCV(RandomForestClassifier(), param_grid, cv=3)
grid.fit(X, y)
print(grid.best_params_)
```

7. Practical Example: Predicting Customer Churn

Scenario:

Predict whether customers will churn using tree-based models.

1. **Prepare Data:**

   python

   ```
   data = pd.read_csv("customer_churn.csv")
   X = data.drop(columns=["Churn"])
   y = data["Churn"]
   ```

2. **Train a Random Forest:**

python

```
rf = RandomForestClassifier(n_estimators=100, random_state=42)
rf.fit(X, y)
```

3. **Train an XGBoost Model:**

python

```
xgb = XGBClassifier(n_estimators=100, learning_rate=0.1, max_depth=3)
xgb.fit(X, y)
```

4. **Evaluate Models:**

python

```
from sklearn.metrics import classification_report

rf_pred = rf.predict(X)
xgb_pred = xgb.predict(X)

print("Random Forest:\n", classification_report(y, rf_pred))
print("XGBoost:\n", classification_report(y, xgb_pred))
```

8. Best Practices

1. **Feature Engineering:** Tree-based models work well with raw data but benefit from feature engineering.

2. **Avoid Overfitting:** Use hyperparameters like max_depth and min_samples_split to control complexity.

3. **Parallelize XGBoost:** Utilize GPUs for faster training on large datasets.

Tree-based models are essential tools in a data scientist's toolkit. Decision trees provide simplicity, random forests offer robustness, and XGBoost delivers state-of-the-art performance. By mastering these techniques, you can tackle a wide range of regression and classification problems effectively.

Chapter 13: Unsupervised Learning and Clustering

Overview

Unsupervised learning identifies patterns and structures in unlabeled data. Clustering is a popular technique in unsupervised learning that groups similar data points into clusters. This chapter explores clustering algorithms such as **K-Means, DBSCAN,** and **Hierarchical Clustering**, along with practical applications.

---

1. Introduction to Clustering

What is Clustering?

Clustering groups data points such that points in the same group (cluster) are more similar to each other than to those in other groups.

Applications of Clustering:

- Customer segmentation.
- Image segmentation.
- Anomaly detection.
- Document clustering.

---

2. K-Means Clustering

What is K-Means?

K-Means is a centroid-based clustering algorithm that divides data into KKK clusters by minimizing the distance between data points and their cluster centroids.

How K-Means Works:

1. Initialize KKK centroids randomly.
2. Assign each point to the nearest centroid.
3. Recompute centroids based on the mean of assigned points.
4. Repeat steps 2-3 until centroids stabilize or a maximum number of iterations is reached.

Steps to Implement K-Means

1. Import Libraries:

python

```python
import numpy as np
import pandas as pd
from sklearn.cluster import KMeans
import matplotlib.pyplot as plt
```

2. Prepare Data:

python

```python
# Example dataset
```

```
data = pd.DataFrame({
    "X": [1, 2, 3, 8, 9, 10],
    "Y": [1, 1, 2, 8, 9, 10]
})
```

3. Apply K-Means:

python

```
kmeans = KMeans(n_clusters=2, random_state=42)
kmeans.fit(data)

# Add cluster labels to data
data["Cluster"] = kmeans.labels_
```

4. Visualize Clusters:

python

```
plt.scatter(data["X"], data["Y"], c=data["Cluster"], cmap="viridis")
plt.scatter(kmeans.cluster_centers_[:, 0], kmeans.cluster_centers_[:, 1], s=200,
c="red", marker="X")
plt.title("K-Means Clustering")
plt.show()
```

---

3. DBSCAN (Density-Based Spatial Clustering of Applications with Noise)

What is DBSCAN?

DBSCAN clusters points based on density, identifying core points (high-density regions), border points (connected to core points), and noise points.

Advantages:

- Detects clusters of arbitrary shapes.
- Handles noise effectively.
- No need to predefine the number of clusters.

Key Parameters:

- **ε\varepsilonε (eps):** Maximum distance between points in a cluster.
- **MinPts:** Minimum number of points in a neighborhood to form a cluster.

Steps to Implement DBSCAN

1. Import Libraries:

python

```
from sklearn.cluster import DBSCAN
```

2. Apply DBSCAN:

python

```
dbscan = DBSCAN(eps=2, min_samples=2)
data["Cluster"] = dbscan.fit_predict(data[["X", "Y"]])
```

3. Visualize Clusters:

python

```
plt.scatter(data["X"], data["Y"], c=data["Cluster"], cmap="viridis")
plt.title("DBSCAN Clustering")
plt.show()
```

---

4. Hierarchical Clustering

What is Hierarchical Clustering?

Hierarchical clustering builds a hierarchy of clusters by either:

- **Agglomerative (bottom-up):** Starting with each point as its own cluster and merging the closest pairs.
- **Divisive (top-down):** Starting with all points in one cluster and splitting recursively.

Dendrogram:

A dendrogram visualizes the clustering hierarchy and helps decide the number of clusters.

Steps to Implement Hierarchical Clustering

1. Import Libraries:

python

```
from scipy.cluster.hierarchy import dendrogram, linkage
from sklearn.cluster import AgglomerativeClustering
```

2. Create Dendrogram:

python

```
linkage_matrix = linkage(data[["X", "Y"]], method="ward")
dendrogram(linkage_matrix)
plt.title("Dendrogram")
plt.show()
```

3. Apply Agglomerative Clustering:

python

```
hierarchical = AgglomerativeClustering(n_clusters=2, linkage="ward")
data["Cluster"] = hierarchical.fit_predict(data[["X", "Y"]])
```

4. Visualize Clusters:

python

```
plt.scatter(data["X"], data["Y"], c=data["Cluster"], cmap="viridis")
plt.title("Hierarchical Clustering")
plt.show()
```

---

5. Evaluating Clustering Performance

1. Silhouette Score:

Measures how similar a data point is to its cluster compared to other clusters.

Silhouette Score=b−amax⁣(a,b)\text{Silhouette Score} = \frac{b - a}{\max(a, b)}Silhouette Score=max(a,b)b−a

Where:

- aaa: Average intra-cluster distance.
- bbb: Average nearest-cluster distance.

python

```
from sklearn.metrics import silhouette_score

score = silhouette_score(data[["X", "Y"]], data["Cluster"])
print(f"Silhouette Score: {score}")
```

2. Elbow Method (K-Means Only):

Plots the sum of squared distances (SSE) to find the optimal KKK.

python

```
sse = []
for k in range(1, 10):
    kmeans = KMeans(n_clusters=k, random_state=42)
    kmeans.fit(data)
    sse.append(kmeans.inertia_)

plt.plot(range(1, 10), sse, marker="o")
plt.title("Elbow Method")
plt.xlabel("Number of Clusters")
plt.ylabel("SSE")
plt.show()
```

6. Comparing Clustering Algorithms

Feature	K-Means	DBSCAN	Hierarchical
Cluster Shape	Spherical	Arbitrary	Arbitrary
Handles Noise	Poor	Excellent	Poor
Scalability	High	Moderate	Low
Number of Clusters	Must be predefined	Determined by density	Determined by dendrogram

7. Practical Example: Customer Segmentation

Scenario:

Segment customers based on their spending habits.

Step 1: Load Data

python

```python
data = pd.DataFrame({
    "Annual_Income": [15, 16, 17, 35, 36, 37, 80, 81, 82],
    "Spending_Score": [39, 81, 6, 6, 77, 40, 29, 4, 70]
})
```

Step 2: Apply K-Means

python

```
kmeans = KMeans(n_clusters=3, random_state=42)
data["Cluster"] = kmeans.fit_predict(data)
```

Step 3: Visualize Clusters

python

```
plt.scatter(data["Annual_Income"], data["Spending_Score"], c=data["Cluster"],
cmap="viridis")
plt.title("Customer Segmentation")
plt.xlabel("Annual Income")
plt.ylabel("Spending Score")
plt.show()
```

8. Best Practices

1. **Scale Data:** Use standardization for algorithms sensitive to feature magnitude.

2. **Experiment with Parameters:** Test different values for ε\varepsilon$\varepsilon$, MinPts (DBSCAN), and KKK (K-Means).

3. **Evaluate Results:** Use silhouette scores or domain knowledge to assess clustering quality.

Clustering is a versatile tool in unsupervised learning for finding hidden patterns in data. By mastering algorithms like K-Means, DBSCAN, and Hierarchical Clustering, you can address a wide range of problems in domains like marketing, image analysis, and anomaly detection.

Chapter 14: Dimensionality Reduction Techniques

Overview

Dimensionality reduction simplifies high-dimensional data into fewer dimensions while retaining essential information. It helps in data compression, visualization, and mitigating the "curse of dimensionality." This chapter focuses on two widely-used techniques: **Principal Component Analysis (PCA)** and **t-Distributed Stochastic Neighbor Embedding (t-SNE).**

---

1. Importance of Dimensionality Reduction

Why Reduce Dimensions?

- **Improves Model Performance:** Reduces noise and redundancy.
- **Eases Visualization:** Enables visualization in 2D or 3D.
- **Mitigates Overfitting:** Reduces the risk of overfitting in high-dimensional datasets.

Applications:

- Preprocessing for machine learning.
- Data compression.

- Visualizing clusters in high-dimensional datasets.

---

2. Principal Component Analysis (PCA)

What is PCA?

PCA transforms data into a new coordinate system by identifying the principal components (directions of maximum variance) and projecting the data onto them.

Steps in PCA:

1. Standardize the data.
2. Compute the covariance matrix.
3. Compute eigenvectors and eigenvalues of the covariance matrix.
4. Select principal components based on eigenvalues.
5. Project data onto the principal components.

Steps to Implement PCA

1. Import Libraries:

python

```
import numpy as np
import pandas as pd
```

```python
from sklearn.decomposition import PCA
from sklearn.preprocessing import StandardScaler
```

2. Prepare Data:

python

```python
# Example dataset
data = pd.DataFrame({
    "Feature1": [2.5, 0.5, 2.2, 1.9, 3.1, 2.3, 2.0, 1.0, 1.5, 1.1],
    "Feature2": [2.4, 0.7, 2.9, 2.2, 3.0, 2.7, 1.6, 1.1, 1.6, 0.9]
})

# Standardize the data
scaler = StandardScaler()
data_scaled = scaler.fit_transform(data)
```

3. Apply PCA:

python

```python
# Perform PCA
pca = PCA(n_components=2)
principal_components = pca.fit_transform(data_scaled)

# Create DataFrame with PCA results
pca_df = pd.DataFrame(data=principal_components, columns=["PC1", "PC2"])
```

4. Visualize Results:

python

```python
import matplotlib.pyplot as plt
```

```
plt.scatter(pca_df["PC1"], pca_df["PC2"])
plt.title("PCA Visualization")
plt.xlabel("Principal Component 1")
plt.ylabel("Principal Component 2")
plt.show()
```

5. Explained Variance:

Evaluate how much variance is captured by each principal component:

python

```
explained_variance = pca.explained_variance_ratio_
print(f"Explained Variance: {explained_variance}")
```

---

3. t-Distributed Stochastic Neighbor Embedding (t-SNE)

What is t-SNE?

t-SNE is a non-linear dimensionality reduction technique, often used for visualizing high-dimensional data in 2D or 3D. It preserves local relationships, making it ideal for identifying clusters.

How t-SNE Works:

1. Maps high-dimensional points into a probability distribution.
2. Maps low-dimensional points to a similar probability distribution.
3. Minimizes the divergence between these distributions.

Steps to Implement t-SNE

1. Import Libraries:

python

```
from sklearn.manifold import TSNE
```

2. Apply t-SNE:

python

```
# Perform t-SNE
tsne = TSNE(n_components=2, perplexity=30, random_state=42)
tsne_results = tsne.fit_transform(data_scaled)

# Create DataFrame with t-SNE results
tsne_df = pd.DataFrame(data=tsne_results, columns=["Dim1", "Dim2"])
```

3. Visualize Results:

python

```
plt.scatter(tsne_df["Dim1"], tsne_df["Dim2"])
plt.title("t-SNE Visualization")
plt.xlabel("Dimension 1")
plt.ylabel("Dimension 2")
plt.show()
```

4. Comparing PCA and t-SNE

Feature	PCA	t-SNE
Type of Reduction	Linear	Non-linear
Preserves Variance	Global	Local
Computational Speed	Fast	Slower
Visualization	Good for high variance	Excellent for clusters

---

5. Evaluating Dimensionality Reduction

Reconstruction Error:

For PCA, calculate how much information is lost:

python

```
reconstructed_data = pca.inverse_transform(principal_components)
error = np.mean((data_scaled - reconstructed_data)**2)
print(f"Reconstruction Error: {error}")
```

Silhouette Score (for Clustering Applications):

Evaluate how well clusters are separated:

python

```
from sklearn.metrics import silhouette_score
```

```
silhouette = silhouette_score(tsne_df, labels)   # 'labels' from a clustering
algorithm
print(f"Silhouette Score: {silhouette}")
```

---

6. Practical Example: Customer Segmentation

Scenario:

Reduce dimensionality of a customer dataset for clustering and visualization.

Step 1: Load Data

python

```
data = pd.DataFrame({
    "Age": [25, 34, 45, 23, 35, 40, 50, 29, 31, 48],
    "Income": [40000, 60000, 80000, 30000, 70000, 75000, 100000, 35000, 45000,
85000],
    "Spending_Score": [60, 70, 80, 50, 90, 85, 40, 55, 65, 75]
})

# Standardize the data
scaler = StandardScaler()
data_scaled = scaler.fit_transform(data)
```

Step 2: Apply PCA

python

```
pca = PCA(n_components=2)
```

```
pca_results = pca.fit_transform(data_scaled)

plt.scatter(pca_results[:, 0], pca_results[:, 1])
plt.title("Customer Segmentation - PCA")
plt.xlabel("PC1")
plt.ylabel("PC2")
plt.show()
```

Step 3: Apply t-SNE

python

```
tsne = TSNE(n_components=2, perplexity=30, random_state=42)
tsne_results = tsne.fit_transform(data_scaled)

plt.scatter(tsne_results[:, 0], tsne_results[:, 1])
plt.title("Customer Segmentation - t-SNE")
plt.xlabel("Dimension 1")
plt.ylabel("Dimension 2")
plt.show()
```

7. Best Practices

1. **Standardize Data:** Ensure all features are on the same scale before applying PCA or t-SNE.

2. **Choose Appropriate Technique:** Use PCA for linear relationships and t-SNE for clustering and visualization.

3. **Experiment with Parameters:** For t-SNE, tune perplexity and learning rate for better results.

Dimensionality reduction techniques like PCA and t-SNE help simplify data while retaining critical information. PCA excels in global variance preservation, whereas t-SNE is ideal for uncovering local patterns and clusters. Mastering these techniques enables better data visualization, compression, and preparation for machine learning tasks.

Chapter 15: Natural Language Processing (NLP)

Overview

Natural Language Processing (NLP) enables machines to understand, interpret, and generate human language. NLP powers applications like chatbots, search engines, and sentiment analysis. This chapter covers essential NLP techniques, including text preprocessing, sentiment analysis, and word embeddings.

---

1. Introduction to NLP

Key Challenges in NLP:

- **Ambiguity:** Words and sentences can have multiple meanings.
- **Context:** The meaning of words depends on their usage.
- **High Dimensionality:** Text data can have a vast number of unique words (features).

Applications of NLP:

- Text classification (e.g., spam detection).
- Sentiment analysis (e.g., product reviews).
- Machine translation (e.g., English to French).

- Information retrieval (e.g., search engines).

---

2. Text Preprocessing

Text preprocessing is the foundational step in NLP to clean and prepare text for analysis or modeling.

Steps in Text Preprocessing:

1. Tokenization:

Splitting text into smaller units like words or sentences.

python

```
from nltk.tokenize import word_tokenize, sent_tokenize

text = "Natural Language Processing is fascinating. Let's learn it!"
word_tokens = word_tokenize(text)
sentence_tokens = sent_tokenize(text)

print("Word Tokens:", word_tokens)
print("Sentence Tokens:", sentence_tokens)
```

2. Lowercasing:

Convert all text to lowercase for uniformity.

python

```
text = text.lower()
```

3. Removing Stopwords:

Eliminate common words that don't contribute much meaning (e.g., "is," "and").

python

```
from nltk.corpus import stopwords

stop_words = set(stopwords.words("english"))
filtered_words = [word for word in word_tokens if word not in stop_words]
print("Filtered Words:", filtered_words)
```

4. Stemming and Lemmatization:

Reduce words to their base forms.

- **Stemming:** Removes suffixes to create root forms.

  python

  ```
  from nltk.stem import PorterStemmer
  stemmer = PorterStemmer()
  stems = [stemmer.stem(word) for word in filtered_words]
  print("Stems:", stems)
  ```

- **Lemmatization:** Converts words to their dictionary forms.

  python

  ```
  from nltk.stem import WordNetLemmatizer
  lemmatizer = WordNetLemmatizer()
  lemmas = [lemmatizer.lemmatize(word) for word in filtered_words]
  ```

```
print("Lemmas:", lemmas)
```

5. Removing Punctuation and Numbers:

Clean text further by removing special characters.

python

```
import re

cleaned_text = re.sub(r"[^a-zA-Z\s]", "", text)
print("Cleaned Text:", cleaned_text)
```

---

3. Sentiment Analysis

Sentiment analysis determines the sentiment (e.g., positive, negative, neutral) of a given text.

Steps to Perform Sentiment Analysis:

1. Import Libraries:

python

```
from sklearn.feature_extraction.text import CountVectorizer
from sklearn.naive_bayes import MultinomialNB
from sklearn.model_selection import train_test_split
from sklearn.metrics import classification_report
```

2. Prepare Data:

python

```
# Example dataset
data = pd.DataFrame({
    "Text": ["I love this product!", "This is terrible.", "Best purchase ever!", "Not
worth the money."],
    "Sentiment": [1, 0, 1, 0]  # 1 = Positive, 0 = Negative
})


X = data["Text"]
y = data["Sentiment"]
```

3. Convert Text to Numeric Data:

Use a bag-of-words model to transform text into feature vectors.

python

```
vectorizer = CountVectorizer()
X_vectorized = vectorizer.fit_transform(X)
```

4. Train a Model:

python

```
X_train, X_test, y_train, y_test = train_test_split(X_vectorized, y, test_size=0.2,
random_state=42)
model = MultinomialNB()
model.fit(X_train, y_train)
```

5. Make Predictions:

python

```
y_pred = model.predict(X_test)
print(classification_report(y_test, y_pred))
```

4. Word Embeddings

Word embeddings represent words as dense vectors in a continuous vector space, capturing semantic meaning and relationships between words.

Popular Word Embedding Techniques:

- **Word2Vec:** Learns word representations using neural networks.
- **GloVe:** Captures global word co-occurrence statistics.
- **FastText:** Extends Word2Vec by considering subwords.

Using Pre-Trained Word Embeddings:

1. Load Pre-Trained Word2Vec (Gensim):

bash

```
pip install gensim
```

python

```
from gensim.models import KeyedVectors

# Load pre-trained Word2Vec model
word2vec = KeyedVectors.load_word2vec_format("GoogleNews-vectors-negative300.bin", binary=True)

# Find word vectors
```

```python
vector = word2vec["king"]
print("Vector for 'king':", vector)
```

```python
# Find similar words
similar_words = word2vec.most_similar("king", topn=5)
print("Similar Words to 'king':", similar_words)
```

2. Train Custom Word2Vec:

python

```python
from gensim.models import Word2Vec
```

```python
# Example sentences
sentences = [["natural", "language", "processing"], ["text", "analysis", "with",
"python"]]
```

```python
# Train Word2Vec
model = Word2Vec(sentences, vector_size=100, window=5, min_count=1,
workers=4)
print("Vector for 'language':", model.wv["language"])
```

---

5. Practical Example: Analyzing Product Reviews

Scenario:

Perform sentiment analysis on customer reviews and visualize word relationships.

Step 1: Load and Preprocess Data

python

```
data = pd.DataFrame({
    "Review": ["Great product!", "Terrible quality.", "Loved it!", "Not good at all."],
    "Sentiment": [1, 0, 1, 0]
})
```

```
# Preprocess reviews
data["Cleaned_Review"] = data["Review"].str.lower().str.replace(r"[^a-z\s]", "")
```

Step 2: Train Word2Vec

python

```
sentences = [review.split() for review in data["Cleaned_Review"]]
model = Word2Vec(sentences, vector_size=50, window=3, min_count=1)
```

Step 3: Visualize Word Embeddings

python

```
from sklearn.manifold import TSNE
import matplotlib.pyplot as plt

words = list(model.wv.index_to_key)
word_vectors = [model.wv[word] for word in words]

tsne = TSNE(n_components=2, random_state=42)
embeddings = tsne.fit_transform(word_vectors)

plt.figure(figsize=(10, 6))
for i, word in enumerate(words):
    plt.scatter(embeddings[i, 0], embeddings[i, 1])
```

```
plt.text(embeddings[i, 0] + 0.01, embeddings[i, 1] + 0.01, word, fontsize=12)
plt.title("Word Embedding Visualization")
plt.show()
```

6. Best Practices

1. **Clean Text Thoroughly:** Ensure consistency and remove irrelevant content.

2. **Leverage Pre-Trained Models:** Save time by using models like Word2Vec or GloVe.

3. **Understand Context:** Use contextual embeddings like BERT for tasks requiring semantic understanding.

NLP is a powerful tool for processing and analyzing text data. By mastering text preprocessing, sentiment analysis, and word embeddings, you can build robust applications for diverse text-related tasks. This chapter equips you with the foundational skills to tackle advanced NLP challenges.

Chapter 16: Understanding Neural Networks

Overview

Neural networks are the foundation of deep learning. They are computational models inspired by the human brain, designed to recognize patterns and solve complex problems. This chapter explores the anatomy of neural networks, focusing on the structure, forward propagation, and backpropagation.

---

1. Anatomy of a Neural Network

Basic Structure:

1. **Input Layer:** Accepts raw data (e.g., images, text, numbers).
2. **Hidden Layers:** Performs computations using neurons (nodes) and activation functions.
3. **Output Layer:** Produces predictions or classifications.

Key Components:

- **Neuron (Node):** The basic unit of a neural network.
- **Weights (WWW):** Determines the influence of an input on the neuron.
- **Bias (bbb):** Adjusts the output independently of the inputs.

- **Activation Function:** Introduces non-linearity, enabling the network to learn complex patterns.

---

2. Forward Propagation

Forward propagation computes the output of a neural network by passing inputs through each layer.

Steps in Forward Propagation:

1. **Weighted Sum:** Each neuron calculates a weighted sum of its inputs: $z=W \cdot X+bz = W \cdot X + bz=W \cdot X+b$
2. **Activation Function:** The activation function transforms zzz to introduce non-linearity: $a=f(z)a = f(z)a=f(z)$

Common Activation Functions:

- **Sigmoid:** Outputs a value between 0 and 1. $f(z)=11+e-zf(z) = \frac{1}{1 + e^{-z}}f(z)=1+e-z1$
- **ReLU (Rectified Linear Unit):** Outputs positive values and zeros otherwise. $f(z)=\max(0,z)f(z) = \max(0, z)f(z)=\max(0,z)$
- **Tanh:** Outputs a value between -1 and 1. $f(z)=\tanh(z)f(z) = \tanh(z)f(z)=\tanh(z)$

Example Forward Pass (Single Layer):

python

```
import numpy as np

# Input and parameters
X = np.array([1, 2]) # Input vector
W = np.array([0.5, -0.6]) # Weights
b = 0.1 # Bias

# Compute weighted sum
z = np.dot(W, X) + b

# Apply ReLU activation
a = max(0, z)
print("Output of the neuron:", a)
```

---

3. Backpropagation

Backpropagation is the process of updating weights and biases in a neural network based on the error (loss) of predictions. It uses the chain rule of calculus to compute gradients efficiently.

Steps in Backpropagation:

1. **Compute Loss:** Measure the difference between predicted and actual values using a loss function:

   $$Loss = \frac{1}{n} \sum (\hat{y} - y)^2$$

2. **Calculate Gradients:** Find the derivative of the loss with respect to weights and biases:

$$\partial Loss \partial W \frac{\partial \text{Loss}}{\partial W} \partial W \partial Loss$$

3. **Update Parameters:** Use gradient descent to update weights and biases:

$$W = W - \eta \cdot \partial Loss \partial WW = W - \eta \cdot \frac{\partial \text{Loss}}{\partial W} W = W - \eta \cdot \partial W \partial Loss$$

Where η\eta$\eta$ is the learning rate.

Example Backpropagation:

python

```
# Example gradient descent update
learning_rate = 0.01
weight = 0.5
gradient = -0.2  # Derivative of loss with respect to weight

# Update weight
weight = weight - learning_rate * gradient
print("Updated weight:", weight)
```

4. Structure of a Neural Network

Fully Connected (Dense) Layer:

Every neuron in one layer is connected to every neuron in the next layer.

Feedforward Neural Network:
Information flows in one direction, from input to output.

Loss Functions:

- **Mean Squared Error (MSE):** For regression tasks. MSE=1n∑i=1n(yi−y^i)2\text{MSE} = \frac{1}{n} \sum_{i=1}^n (y_i - \hat{y}_i)^2MSE=n1i=1∑n(yi−y^i)2
- **Binary Cross-Entropy:** For binary classification. Loss=−1n∑i=1n[yilog⁡(y^i)+(1−yi)log⁡(1−y^i)]\text{Loss} = - \frac{1}{n} \sum_{i=1}^n [y_i \log(\hat{y}_i) + (1 - y_i) \log(1 - \hat{y}_i)]Loss=−n1i=1∑n[yilog(y^i)+(1−yi)log(1−y^i)]
- **Categorical Cross-Entropy:** For multi-class classification.

---

5. Building a Neural Network in Python

Using NumPy:
python

```
# Input, weights, and bias
X = np.array([1, 0]) # Input
W = np.array([[0.2, 0.8], [0.5, -0.1]]) # Weights
```

```python
b = np.array([0.1, 0.2])  # Bias

# Forward propagation
z = np.dot(X, W) + b
a = np.maximum(0, z)  # ReLU activation
print("Output:", a)
```

Using TensorFlow/Keras:

bash

```
pip install tensorflow
python
```

```python
from tensorflow.keras.models import Sequential
from tensorflow.keras.layers import Dense

# Create a neural network
model = Sequential([
    Dense(32, input_dim=10, activation="relu"),  # Hidden layer
    Dense(1, activation="sigmoid")          # Output layer
])

# Compile the model
model.compile(optimizer="adam",                    loss="binary_crossentropy",
metrics=["accuracy"])

# Train the model
X = np.random.rand(100, 10)  # Random input data
y = np.random.randint(0, 2, 100)  # Random binary labels
model.fit(X, y, epochs=10, batch_size=10)
```

6. Practical Example: Predicting Binary Outcomes

Scenario:

Predict whether customers will churn based on their features.

Step 1: Prepare Data

python

```
from sklearn.datasets import make_classification
from sklearn.model_selection import train_test_split

# Generate synthetic data
X, y = make_classification(n_samples=1000, n_features=10, random_state=42)
X_train, X_test, y_train, y_test = train_test_split(X, y, test_size=0.2, random_state=42)
```

Step 2: Build Neural Network

python

```
from tensorflow.keras.models import Sequential
from tensorflow.keras.layers import Dense

model = Sequential([
    Dense(64, input_dim=10, activation="relu"),
    Dense(1, activation="sigmoid")
])
```

```
model.compile(optimizer="adam",                loss="binary_crossentropy",
metrics=["accuracy"])
```

Step 3: Train and Evaluate

python

```
model.fit(X_train, y_train, epochs=10, batch_size=32)
loss, accuracy = model.evaluate(X_test, y_test)
print(f"Test Accuracy: {accuracy}")
```

---

7. Best Practices

1. **Choose Activation Functions Wisely:** Use ReLU for hidden layers and softmax or sigmoid for output layers.
2. **Normalize Input Data:** Scale inputs to improve convergence.
3. **Monitor Overfitting:** Use regularization techniques (e.g., dropout) and validation sets.

Understanding neural networks' anatomy, forward propagation, and backpropagation is essential for mastering deep learning. By implementing these concepts, you can build and train neural networks for diverse tasks, laying the groundwork for advanced architectures like convolutional and recurrent neural networks.

Chapter 17: Building Deep Learning Models with TensorFlow and PyTorch

Overview

TensorFlow and PyTorch are two of the most popular frameworks for deep learning. They provide robust tools for creating, training, and deploying deep learning models. This chapter explores how to build deep learning models using both frameworks, focusing on key concepts and practical implementation.

---

1. Introduction to TensorFlow and PyTorch

TensorFlow:

- Developed by Google.
- Offers high-level APIs like Keras for quick prototyping.
- Optimized for production deployment with TensorFlow Serving and TensorFlow Lite.

PyTorch:

- Developed by Facebook.
- Emphasizes dynamic computation graphs, making debugging and experimentation easier.
- Popular in research for its flexibility.

2. Setting Up TensorFlow and PyTorch

Installation:

bash

```
pip install tensorflow
pip install torch torchvision
```

3. Building Models with TensorFlow

Steps to Build a Deep Learning Model:

1. Import Required Libraries:

python

```
import tensorflow as tf
from tensorflow.keras.models import Sequential
from tensorflow.keras.layers import Dense
```

2. Create the Model:

python

```
model = Sequential([
    Dense(64, input_dim=10, activation="relu"),  # Hidden layer
    Dense(32, activation="relu"),            # Hidden layer
    Dense(1, activation="sigmoid")           # Output layer
])
```

3. Compile the Model:

python

```
model.compile(optimizer="adam", loss="binary_crossentropy", metrics=["accuracy"])
```

4. Train the Model:

python

```
# Generate synthetic data
import numpy as np
X_train = np.random.rand(1000, 10)
y_train = np.random.randint(0, 2, size=1000)

model.fit(X_train, y_train, epochs=10, batch_size=32)
```

5. Evaluate the Model:

python

```
X_test = np.random.rand(200, 10)
y_test = np.random.randint(0, 2, size=200)

loss, accuracy = model.evaluate(X_test, y_test)
print(f"Test Accuracy: {accuracy}")
```

---

4. Building Models with PyTorch

Steps to Build a Deep Learning Model:

1. Import Required Libraries:

python

```
import torch
import torch.nn as nn
import torch.optim as optim
```

2. Define the Model:

python

```
class SimpleNN(nn.Module):
    def __init__(self):
        super(SimpleNN, self).__init__()
        self.fc1 = nn.Linear(10, 64)  # Hidden layer
        self.fc2 = nn.Linear(64, 32) # Hidden layer
        self.fc3 = nn.Linear(32, 1)  # Output layer
        self.sigmoid = nn.Sigmoid()

    def forward(self, x):
        x = torch.relu(self.fc1(x))
        x = torch.relu(self.fc2(x))
        x = self.sigmoid(self.fc3(x))
        return x


model = SimpleNN()
```

3. Define the Loss Function and Optimizer:

python

```
criterion = nn.BCELoss()  # Binary Cross-Entropy Loss
optimizer = optim.Adam(model.parameters(), lr=0.001)
```

4. Train the Model:

python

```python
# Generate synthetic data
X_train = torch.rand(1000, 10)
y_train = torch.randint(0, 2, (1000, 1)).float()

for epoch in range(10):  # Number of epochs
    optimizer.zero_grad()  # Reset gradients
    outputs = model(X_train)  # Forward pass
    loss = criterion(outputs, y_train)  # Compute loss
    loss.backward()  # Backward pass
    optimizer.step()  # Update weights
    print(f"Epoch {epoch+1}, Loss: {loss.item()}")
```

5. Evaluate the Model:

python

```python
X_test = torch.rand(200, 10)
y_test = torch.randint(0, 2, (200, 1)).float()

with torch.no_grad():
    predictions = model(X_test)
    predictions = (predictions > 0.5).float()
    accuracy = (predictions == y_test).sum() / y_test.size(0)
    print(f"Test Accuracy: {accuracy.item()}")
```

---

5. Comparing TensorFlow and PyTorch

Feature	TensorFlow	PyTorch
Ease of Use	High (Keras API)	Moderate
Flexibility	Moderate	High
Production Deployment	Excellent	Limited (requires ONNX)
Debugging	Moderate	Excellent (dynamic graphs)
Popularity in Research	High	Very High

6. Practical Example: MNIST Digit Classification

Using TensorFlow:

python

```
from tensorflow.keras.datasets import mnist
from tensorflow.keras.utils import to_categorical

# Load dataset
(X_train, y_train), (X_test, y_test) = mnist.load_data()
X_train, X_test = X_train / 255.0, X_test / 255.0  # Normalize
```

```python
X_train = X_train.reshape(-1, 28*28)
X_test = X_test.reshape(-1, 28*28)
y_train = to_categorical(y_train)
y_test = to_categorical(y_test)

# Build model
model = Sequential([
    Dense(128, input_dim=784, activation="relu"),
    Dense(64, activation="relu"),
    Dense(10, activation="softmax")
])

model.compile(optimizer="adam",                loss="categorical_crossentropy",
metrics=["accuracy"])
model.fit(X_train, y_train, epochs=5, batch_size=32)
model.evaluate(X_test, y_test)
```

Using PyTorch:

python

```python
from torchvision import datasets, transforms
from torch.utils.data import DataLoader

# Load dataset
transform = transforms.ToTensor()
train_dataset = datasets.MNIST(root="./data", train=True, transform=transform,
download=True)
test_dataset = datasets.MNIST(root="./data", train=False, transform=transform)

train_loader = DataLoader(train_dataset, batch_size=32, shuffle=True)
test_loader = DataLoader(test_dataset, batch_size=32)
```

```python
# Define model
class MNISTModel(nn.Module):
    def __init__(self):
        super(MNISTModel, self).__init__()
        self.fc1 = nn.Linear(28*28, 128)
        self.fc2 = nn.Linear(128, 64)
        self.fc3 = nn.Linear(64, 10)

    def forward(self, x):
        x = x.view(-1, 28*28)
        x = torch.relu(self.fc1(x))
        x = torch.relu(self.fc2(x))
        x = self.fc3(x)
        return x

model = MNISTModel()

# Loss and optimizer
criterion = nn.CrossEntropyLoss()
optimizer = optim.Adam(model.parameters(), lr=0.001)

# Train model
for epoch in range(5):
    for images, labels in train_loader:
        optimizer.zero_grad()
        outputs = model(images)
        loss = criterion(outputs, labels)
        loss.backward()
        optimizer.step()
```

```
    print(f"Epoch {epoch+1}, Loss: {loss.item()}")

# Evaluate model
correct = 0
total = 0
with torch.no_grad():
    for images, labels in test_loader:
        outputs = model(images)
        _, predicted = torch.max(outputs, 1)
        total += labels.size(0)
        correct += (predicted == labels).sum().item()

print(f"Test Accuracy: {correct / total}")
```

7. Best Practices

1. **Data Preparation:** Ensure proper normalization and augmentation for better performance.

2. **Learning Rate Tuning:** Use techniques like learning rate schedulers for optimal training.

3. **Regularization:** Apply dropout or weight decay to prevent overfitting.

TensorFlow and PyTorch are versatile frameworks for building and training deep learning models. TensorFlow excels in production, while PyTorch is favored for research. Mastering both allows you to choose the right tool for your project and effectively tackle deep learning challenges.

Chapter 18: Convolutional Neural Networks (CNNs)

Overview

Convolutional Neural Networks (CNNs) are deep learning models designed to process grid-like data, such as images. They are the backbone of many computer vision tasks, including image classification and object detection. This chapter explores CNNs, their architecture, and their application to real-world problems.

---

1. What are Convolutional Neural Networks?

Key Features of CNNs:

- **Local Connectivity:** Neurons are connected to local regions of the input.
- **Shared Weights:** Reduces the number of parameters, enhancing efficiency.
- **Translation Invariance:** Recognizes patterns regardless of their position in the input.

Applications of CNNs:

- Image classification (e.g., recognizing handwritten digits).
- Object detection (e.g., identifying objects in photos).

- Semantic segmentation (e.g., pixel-level classification of images).

---

2. Architecture of CNNs

Key Layers in CNNs:

1. **Convolutional Layer:**
   - Extracts features by applying filters (kernels) to the input.
   - Output:

     Feature Map=(Input*Kernel)+Bias\text{Feature Map} = (\text{Input} \ast \text{Kernel}) + \text{Bias}Feature Map=(Input*Kernel)+Bias

2. **Activation Layer:**
   - Introduces non-linearity using functions like ReLU.

3. **Pooling Layer:**
   - Reduces spatial dimensions (down-sampling) to make the network computationally efficient.
   - Common methods: Max pooling, Average pooling.

4. **Fully Connected Layer:**
   - Flattens the feature maps and connects them to the output layer for predictions.

5. **Dropout Layer:**

o   Prevents overfitting by randomly setting a fraction of inputs to zero during training.

---

3. Building a CNN with TensorFlow/Keras

Steps to Build a CNN for Image Classification:

1. Import Libraries:

python

```
import tensorflow as tf
from tensorflow.keras.models import Sequential
from tensorflow.keras.layers import Conv2D, MaxPooling2D, Flatten, Dense, Dropout
from tensorflow.keras.datasets import mnist
from tensorflow.keras.utils import to_categorical
```

2. Load and Preprocess Data:

python

```
# Load MNIST dataset
(X_train, y_train), (X_test, y_test) = mnist.load_data()

# Normalize data
X_train = X_train / 255.0
X_test = X_test / 255.0

# Reshape data for CNN
```

```python
X_train = X_train.reshape(-1, 28, 28, 1)
X_test = X_test.reshape(-1, 28, 28, 1)

# One-hot encode labels
y_train = to_categorical(y_train)
y_test = to_categorical(y_test)
```

3. Build the CNN:

python

```python
model = Sequential([
    Conv2D(32, (3, 3), activation="relu", input_shape=(28, 28, 1)),
    MaxPooling2D((2, 2)),
    Conv2D(64, (3, 3), activation="relu"),
    MaxPooling2D((2, 2)),
    Flatten(),
    Dense(128, activation="relu"),
    Dropout(0.5),
    Dense(10, activation="softmax")
])
```

4. Compile the Model:

python

```python
model.compile(optimizer="adam", loss="categorical_crossentropy", metrics=["accuracy"])
```

5. Train the Model:

python

```
model.fit(X_train, y_train, epochs=5, batch_size=64, validation_data=(X_test, y_test))
```

6. Evaluate the Model:

python

```
loss, accuracy = model.evaluate(X_test, y_test)
print(f"Test Accuracy: {accuracy}")
```

---

4. Building a CNN with PyTorch

Steps to Build a CNN for Image Classification:

1. Import Libraries:

python

```
import torch
import torch.nn as nn
import torch.optim as optim
from torchvision import datasets, transforms
from torch.utils.data import DataLoader
```

2. Load and Preprocess Data:

python

```
# Transform dataset
transform = transforms.Compose([
    transforms.ToTensor(),
    transforms.Normalize((0.5,), (0.5,))
])
```

```python
# Load dataset
train_dataset = datasets.MNIST(root="./data", train=True, transform=transform,
download=True)
test_dataset = datasets.MNIST(root="./data", train=False, transform=transform)

train_loader = DataLoader(train_dataset, batch_size=64, shuffle=True)
test_loader = DataLoader(test_dataset, batch_size=64)
```

3. Define the CNN:

python

```python
class CNN(nn.Module):
    def __init__(self):
        super(CNN, self).__init__()
        self.conv1 = nn.Conv2d(1, 32, kernel_size=3)
        self.pool = nn.MaxPool2d(2, 2)
        self.conv2 = nn.Conv2d(32, 64, kernel_size=3)
        self.fc1 = nn.Linear(64 * 5 * 5, 128)
        self.fc2 = nn.Linear(128, 10)

    def forward(self, x):
        x = self.pool(torch.relu(self.conv1(x)))
        x = self.pool(torch.relu(self.conv2(x)))
        x = x.view(-1, 64 * 5 * 5)
        x = torch.relu(self.fc1(x))
        x = self.fc2(x)
        return x

model = CNN()
```

4. Define Loss and Optimizer:

python

```python
criterion = nn.CrossEntropyLoss()
optimizer = optim.Adam(model.parameters(), lr=0.001)
```

5. Train the Model:

python

```python
for epoch in range(5):  # Number of epochs
    for images, labels in train_loader:
        optimizer.zero_grad()  # Reset gradients
        outputs = model(images)  # Forward pass
        loss = criterion(outputs, labels)  # Compute loss
        loss.backward()  # Backward pass
        optimizer.step()  # Update weights
    print(f"Epoch {epoch+1}, Loss: {loss.item()}")
```

6. Evaluate the Model:

python

```python
correct = 0
total = 0
with torch.no_grad():
    for images, labels in test_loader:
        outputs = model(images)
        _, predicted = torch.max(outputs, 1)
        total += labels.size(0)
        correct += (predicted == labels).sum().item()

print(f"Test Accuracy: {correct / total}")
```

5. Object Detection with CNNs

Object detection involves identifying and localizing objects in an image. Advanced architectures like **YOLO** and **Faster R-CNN** build on CNNs for this task.

Steps for Object Detection:

1. Extract features using CNNs.
2. Use bounding boxes for localization.
3. Classify the objects within the bounding boxes.

6. Best Practices for CNNs

1. **Data Augmentation:** Use techniques like flipping, cropping, and rotation to increase dataset diversity.
2. **Regularization:** Apply dropout to reduce overfitting.
3. **Transfer Learning:** Use pre-trained models like VGG, ResNet, or Inception to save time and improve accuracy.
4. **Optimize Hyperparameters:** Experiment with filter sizes, strides, and learning rates.

Convolutional Neural Networks are the cornerstone of modern computer vision tasks. By mastering CNNs, you can tackle challenges like image classification, object detection, and beyond. TensorFlow and PyTorch provide robust frameworks to implement and deploy CNNs efficiently.

Chapter 19: Recurrent Neural Networks (RNNs)

Overview

Recurrent Neural Networks (RNNs) are designed for sequential data, such as time-series data, text, and speech. Unlike traditional feedforward neural networks, RNNs maintain a memory of previous inputs, making them ideal for tasks where context and sequence matter.

1. What are RNNs?

Key Features of RNNs:

- **Sequential Memory:** Maintains a hidden state that captures information about previous inputs.
- **Recurrent Connections:** Allows feedback loops, making RNNs suitable for processing sequences.

Applications of RNNs:

- **Time-Series Analysis:** Stock price prediction, weather forecasting.
- **Natural Language Processing (NLP):** Text generation, machine translation, sentiment analysis.

- **Speech Processing:** Speech recognition, audio generation.

---

2. Anatomy of an RNN

Core Components:

1. **Input:** Sequence data processed one element at a time.
2. **Hidden State:** Captures information from previous time steps.
3. **Output:** Prediction or transformation of the sequence.

Mathematical Representation:

- Hidden state at time ttt: $ht=f(Wh \cdot ht-1+Wx \cdot xt+b)h\_t = f(W\_h \cdot h\_{t-1} + W\_x \cdot x\_t + b)ht=f(Wh \cdot ht-1+Wx \cdot xt+b)$

- Output at time ttt: $yt=g(Wy \cdot ht+by)y\_t = g(W\_y \cdot h\_t + b\_y)yt=g(Wy \cdot ht+by)$

Where:

- fff: Activation function (e.g., tanh or ReLU).
- ggg: Output activation function (e.g., softmax).

---

3. Challenges with RNNs

Vanishing and Exploding Gradients:

- Gradients can become too small (vanishing) or too large (exploding) during backpropagation.
- Solutions include:
    - **Gradient Clipping:** Limit gradient magnitude.
    - **Advanced Architectures:** Long Short-Term Memory (LSTM) and Gated Recurrent Unit (GRU).

---

4. Advanced RNN Architectures

Long Short-Term Memory (LSTM):

LSTMs address the vanishing gradient problem with a memory cell and gates:

1. **Forget Gate:** Decides what information to discard.
2. **Input Gate:** Decides what new information to store.
3. **Output Gate:** Decides what to output from the memory cell.

Gated Recurrent Unit (GRU):

Simpler than LSTMs, GRUs combine the forget and input gates into a single update gate.

---

5. Building RNNs with TensorFlow/Keras

Steps to Build an RNN for Time-Series Prediction:

1. Import Libraries:

python

```
import tensorflow as tf
from tensorflow.keras.models import Sequential
from tensorflow.keras.layers import SimpleRNN, LSTM, GRU, Dense
import numpy as np
```

2. Generate Sequential Data:

python

```
# Generate synthetic time-series data
X = np.linspace(0, 100, 1000)
y = np.sin(X)

# Prepare data
window_size = 20
X_data = np.array([y[i:i+window_size] for i in range(len(y) - window_size)])
y_data = y[window_size:]

X_train = X_data[:, :, np.newaxis]
y_train = y_data
```

3. Build the RNN:

python

```
model = Sequential([
```

```
SimpleRNN(50, activation="tanh", input_shape=(window_size, 1)),
Dense(1)
])
```

4. Compile and Train:

python

```
model.compile(optimizer="adam", loss="mse")
model.fit(X_train, y_train, epochs=10, batch_size=32)
```

---

6. Building RNNs with PyTorch

Steps to Build an RNN for Time-Series Prediction:

1. Import Libraries:

python

```
import torch
import torch.nn as nn
import torch.optim as optim
```

2. Define the RNN:

python

```
class RNN(nn.Module):
    def __init__(self, input_size, hidden_size, output_size):
        super(RNN, self).__init__()
        self.rnn = nn.RNN(input_size, hidden_size, batch_first=True)
        self.fc = nn.Linear(hidden_size, output_size)
```

```python
def forward(self, x):
    out, _ = self.rnn(x)
    out = self.fc(out[:, -1, :])  # Use the last time step
    return out


model = RNN(input_size=1, hidden_size=50, output_size=1)
```

3. Define Loss and Optimizer:

python

```python
criterion = nn.MSELoss()
optimizer = optim.Adam(model.parameters(), lr=0.001)
```

4. Train the RNN:

python

```python
# Convert data to PyTorch tensors
X_train = torch.tensor(X_train, dtype=torch.float32)
y_train = torch.tensor(y_train, dtype=torch.float32)

for epoch in range(10):
    optimizer.zero_grad()
    outputs = model(X_train)
    loss = criterion(outputs.squeeze(), y_train)
    loss.backward()
    optimizer.step()
    print(f"Epoch {epoch+1}, Loss: {loss.item()}")
```

---

7. NLP Applications with RNNs

Text Generation Example (Keras):

1. Prepare Data:

python

```python
text = "hello world"
chars = sorted(list(set(text)))
char_to_index = {char: i for i, char in enumerate(chars)}
index_to_char = {i: char for char, i in char_to_index.items()}

# Convert text to sequences
sequence_length = 5
X = []
y = []
for i in range(len(text) - sequence_length):
    X.append([char_to_index[char] for char in text[i:i+sequence_length]])
    y.append(char_to_index[text[i+sequence_length]])

X = np.array(X)
y = np.array(y)
```

2. Build the Model:

python

```python
model = Sequential([
    LSTM(50, input_shape=(sequence_length, len(chars))),
    Dense(len(chars), activation="softmax")
])
```

3. Compile and Train:

python

```
model.compile(optimizer="adam", loss="sparse_categorical_crossentropy")
model.fit(X, y, epochs=20, batch_size=1)
```

4. Generate Text:

python

```
seed = "hello"
for _ in range(5):
    seed_input = np.array([[char_to_index[char] for char in seed]])
    seed_input = seed_input.reshape((1, sequence_length, len(chars)))
    prediction = model.predict(seed_input, verbose=0)
    next_char = index_to_char[np.argmax(prediction)]
    seed += next_char
print(seed)
```

---

8. Best Practices for RNNs

1. **Use Advanced Architectures:** Prefer LSTMs or GRUs for better performance on long sequences.
2. **Batch Sequences:** Use sequences of equal length or padding for batch processing.
3. **Tune Hyperparameters:** Experiment with sequence length, hidden units, and learning rates.

RNNs are powerful tools for sequential data analysis. By leveraging advanced architectures like LSTMs and GRUs, you can effectively handle tasks in time-series prediction and NLP. TensorFlow and PyTorch provide flexible frameworks to build, train, and deploy RNN models efficiently.

Chapter 20: Transfer Learning and Pre-Trained Models

Overview

Transfer learning leverages pre-trained models to save time and computational resources, enabling faster training and better performance, especially on small datasets. This chapter explores the concept of transfer learning, its benefits, and how to implement it using popular frameworks and pre-trained models.

---

1. What is Transfer Learning?

Definition:

Transfer learning involves using a model trained on a large dataset for a similar task on a smaller dataset. Instead of training a model from scratch, a pre-trained model serves as a starting point.

Key Advantages:

- Reduces training time.
- Improves performance on small datasets.
- Reduces the need for extensive labeled data.
- Leverages state-of-the-art architectures and weights.

Applications:

- Image classification (e.g., leveraging models like VGG, ResNet).
- NLP (e.g., using BERT, GPT, or Transformer-based models).
- Object detection (e.g., YOLO, Faster R-CNN).

---

2. Pre-Trained Models

Popular Pre-Trained Models for Images:

1. **VGG (Visual Geometry Group):**
   o Deep, simple architecture.
   o Suitable for fine-tuning.

2. **ResNet (Residual Network):**
   o Introduced skip connections to address vanishing gradients.
   o Excellent for large datasets and high accuracy.

3. **Inception (GoogleNet):**
   o Multi-scale feature extraction with inception modules.

4. **MobileNet:**
   o Lightweight architecture optimized for mobile and embedded systems.

Popular Pre-Trained Models for NLP:

1. **BERT (Bidirectional Encoder Representations from Transformers):**
    - Pre-trained for masked language modeling and next sentence prediction.
    - Ideal for classification, translation, and question-answering tasks.

2. **GPT (Generative Pre-trained Transformer):**
    - Focused on text generation and completion.

3. **T5 (Text-to-Text Transfer Transformer):**
    - Converts every NLP problem into a text-to-text format.

---

3. Transfer Learning Workflow

Steps for Transfer Learning:

1. **Choose a Pre-Trained Model:**
    - Select a model based on the task and dataset (e.g., ResNet for images, BERT for text).

2. **Freeze Layers:**
    - Retain pre-trained weights in initial layers to preserve learned features.

3. **Add Custom Layers:**
    - Modify the model's output layers to match the target task.

4. Fine-Tune the Model:

○ Train the new layers while optionally unfreezing and fine-tuning specific pre-trained layers.

---

4. Transfer Learning for Image Classification

Example with TensorFlow/Keras:

1. Import Libraries:

python

```
import tensorflow as tf
from tensorflow.keras.applications import ResNet50
from tensorflow.keras.models import Sequential
from tensorflow.keras.layers import Dense, Flatten
from tensorflow.keras.preprocessing.image import ImageDataGenerator
```

2. Load Pre-Trained Model:

python

```
base_model    =    ResNet50(weights="imagenet",    include_top=False,
input_shape=(224, 224, 3))
base_model.trainable = False  # Freeze pre-trained layers
```

3. Build Custom Model:

python

```
model = Sequential([
```

```
    base_model,
    Flatten(),
    Dense(128, activation="relu"),
    Dense(10, activation="softmax")  # Adjust output layer for the task
])
```

4. Compile and Train:

python

```
model.compile(optimizer="adam",            loss="categorical_crossentropy",
metrics=["accuracy"])
```

```
# Data augmentation
datagen    =    ImageDataGenerator(rescale=1./255,    rotation_range=20,
width_shift_range=0.2, height_shift_range=0.2, horizontal_flip=True)
train_data    =    datagen.flow_from_directory("path_to_train_data",
target_size=(224, 224), batch_size=32, class_mode="categorical")
```

```
model.fit(train_data, epochs=10)
```

5. Fine-Tune Specific Layers:

python

```
# Unfreeze some layers in the base model
base_model.trainable = True
for layer in base_model.layers[:-10]:  # Freeze earlier layers
    layer.trainable = False
```

```
model.compile(optimizer=tf.keras.optimizers.Adam(1e-5),
loss="categorical_crossentropy", metrics=["accuracy"])
model.fit(train_data, epochs=5)
```

5. Transfer Learning for NLP

Example with Hugging Face Transformers:

1. Install Transformers:

bash

pip install transformers

2. Load a Pre-Trained Model:

python

```python
from transformers import BertTokenizer, BertForSequenceClassification
from transformers import Trainer, TrainingArguments

# Load tokenizer and model
tokenizer = BertTokenizer.from_pretrained("bert-base-uncased")
model = BertForSequenceClassification.from_pretrained("bert-base-uncased",
num_labels=2)
```

3. Prepare Data:

python

```python
# Example data
texts = ["I love programming!", "This is a bad experience."]
labels = [1, 0]  # Positive: 1, Negative: 0

# Tokenize data
```

```python
encoded_inputs = tokenizer(texts, padding=True, truncation=True,
max_length=512, return_tensors="pt")
```

4. Define Trainer and Train:

python

```python
# Define training arguments
training_args = TrainingArguments(
    output_dir="./results",
    num_train_epochs=3,
    per_device_train_batch_size=8,
    evaluation_strategy="epoch",
    save_strategy="epoch",
    logging_dir="./logs",
)


# Define Trainer
from torch.utils.data import Dataset

class CustomDataset(Dataset):
    def __init__(self, encodings, labels):
        self.encodings = encodings
        self.labels = labels

    def __len__(self):
        return len(self.labels)

    def __getitem__(self, idx):
        return {key: val[idx] for key, val in self.encodings.items()}, self.labels[idx]

dataset = CustomDataset(encoded_inputs, labels)
```

```
trainer = Trainer(
    model=model,
    args=training_args,
    train_dataset=dataset,
)


trainer.train()
```

---

6. Practical Example: Fine-Tuning BERT for Sentiment Analysis

Steps:

1. **Load Pre-Trained BERT.**
2. **Add a classification head for binary sentiment analysis.**
3. **Fine-tune the model on a labeled sentiment dataset like IMDb.**

---

7. Best Practices for Transfer Learning

1. **Start with Pre-Trained Weights:** Use models trained on large, similar datasets.
2. **Freeze Layers Initially:** Prevent overfitting by freezing most layers during the initial training phase.

3. **Fine-Tune Gradually:** Unfreeze and fine-tune specific layers for better adaptation to the target task.

4. **Data Augmentation:** Enhance smaller datasets with techniques like cropping, flipping, or noise injection.

Transfer learning accelerates model development by leveraging pre-trained models, saving time and computational resources. Whether in computer vision or NLP, frameworks like TensorFlow, PyTorch, and Hugging Face simplify transfer learning, enabling you to achieve state-of-the-art performance with minimal effort.

Chapter 21: Generative Models and GANs

Overview

Generative models aim to create new data similar to the training data, making them essential for applications like image generation, style transfer, and data augmentation. Among generative models, **Generative Adversarial Networks (GANs)** have revolutionized deep learning with their ability to generate highly realistic outputs. This chapter introduces GANs, their architecture, and practical applications.

---

1. What are Generative Models?

Definition:

Generative models learn the underlying distribution of training data to generate new, similar data points.

Types of Generative Models:

1. **Autoregressive Models:** Predict the next data point in a sequence (e.g., PixelRNN, GPT).

2. **Variational Autoencoders (VAEs):** Learn a compressed latent representation of data.

3. **Generative Adversarial Networks (GANs):** Employ adversarial training to generate realistic data.

---

2. What are GANs?

Introduction to GANs:

Proposed by Ian Goodfellow in 2014, GANs consist of two neural networks, a **Generator** and a **Discriminator**, that compete against each other in a zero-sum game.

Key Components:

1. **Generator (G):**
   - Takes random noise as input and generates synthetic data.
   - Goal: Fool the discriminator by creating realistic data.
2. **Discriminator (D):**
   - Takes real or generated data as input and predicts whether it's real or fake.
   - Goal: Accurately classify real and fake data.

---

3. How GANs Work

Adversarial Training:

1. The generator learns to create data that looks real.

2. The discriminator learns to differentiate between real and generated data.

3. The generator and discriminator are updated alternately:

   o Generator minimizes the discriminator's ability to distinguish real from fake.

   o Discriminator maximizes its ability to distinguish real from fake.

Loss Functions:

- **Discriminator   Loss:**
  LD=−Ex~preal[log▦(D(x))]−Ez~pz[log▦(1−D(G(z)))]L_D = -\mathbb{E}_{x \sim p_{\text{real}}}[\log(D(x))] - \mathbb{E}_{z \sim p_z}[\log(1 - D(G(z)))]LD=−Ex~preal[log(D(x))]−Ez~pz[log(1−D(G(z)))]

- **Generator Loss:** LG=−Ez~pz[log▦(D(G(z)))]L_G = -\mathbb{E}_{z \sim p_z}[\log(D(G(z)))]LG=−Ez~pz[log(D(G(z)))]

---

4. Building GANs with TensorFlow/Keras

Steps to Build a Simple GAN for Image Generation:

1. Import Libraries:

python

```python
import tensorflow as tf
from tensorflow.keras.models import Sequential, Model
from tensorflow.keras.layers import Dense, Flatten, Reshape, BatchNormalization, LeakyReLU
import numpy as np
```

2. Define the Generator:

python

```python
def build_generator():
    model = Sequential([
        Dense(128, activation="relu", input_dim=100),
        BatchNormalization(),
        LeakyReLU(0.2),
        Dense(256, activation="relu"),
        BatchNormalization(),
        LeakyReLU(0.2),
        Dense(784, activation="tanh"),  # For MNIST (28x28 flattened to 784)
        Reshape((28, 28, 1))
    ])
    return model


generator = build_generator()
```

3. Define the Discriminator:

python

```python
def build_discriminator():
    model = Sequential([
```

```
    Flatten(input_shape=(28, 28, 1)),
    Dense(256),
    LeakyReLU(0.2),
    Dense(128),
    LeakyReLU(0.2),
    Dense(1, activation="sigmoid")  # Binary classification
])
return model
```

```
discriminator = build_discriminator()
discriminator.compile(optimizer="adam",            loss="binary_crossentropy",
metrics=["accuracy"])
```

4. Combine Generator and Discriminator:

python

```
def build_gan(generator, discriminator):
    discriminator.trainable = False
    model = Sequential([generator, discriminator])
    return model
```

```
gan = build_gan(generator, discriminator)
gan.compile(optimizer="adam", loss="binary_crossentropy")
```

5. Train the GAN:

python

```
# Load and preprocess data
(X_train, _), _ = tf.keras.datasets.mnist.load_data()
X_train = (X_train / 127.5) - 1  # Normalize to [-1, 1]
X_train = np.expand_dims(X_train, axis=-1)
```

```python
# Training parameters
epochs = 10000
batch_size = 64
latent_dim = 100

for epoch in range(epochs):
    # Train discriminator
    idx = np.random.randint(0, X_train.shape[0], batch_size)
    real_images = X_train[idx]
    noise = np.random.normal(0, 1, (batch_size, latent_dim))
    fake_images = generator.predict(noise)

    real_labels = np.ones((batch_size, 1))
    fake_labels = np.zeros((batch_size, 1))

    d_loss_real = discriminator.train_on_batch(real_images, real_labels)
    d_loss_fake = discriminator.train_on_batch(fake_images, fake_labels)
    d_loss = 0.5 * np.add(d_loss_real, d_loss_fake)

    # Train generator
    noise = np.random.normal(0, 1, (batch_size, latent_dim))
    valid_labels = np.ones((batch_size, 1))  # Trick discriminator
    g_loss = gan.train_on_batch(noise, valid_labels)

    if epoch % 1000 == 0:
        print(f"{epoch} [D loss: {d_loss[0]} | D accuracy: {100 * d_loss[1]}] [G
loss: {g_loss}]")
```

5. Applications of GANs

1. Image Generation:

- Generate realistic images from random noise (e.g., DCGAN).

2. Data Augmentation:

- Create synthetic data to augment training datasets (e.g., GANs for medical imaging).

3. Style Transfer:

- Combine styles of different images (e.g., StyleGAN).

4. Super-Resolution:

- Enhance image resolution (e.g., SRGAN).

5. Anomaly Detection:

- Use GANs to model normal data distribution and detect anomalies.

---

6. Variations of GANs

1. Deep Convolutional GAN (DCGAN):

Uses convolutional layers to improve the quality of generated images.

2. Conditional GAN (cGAN):

Incorporates additional input (e.g., labels) to control output generation.

3. Wasserstein GAN (WGAN):

Uses the Wasserstein distance to stabilize training.

---

7. Best Practices for Training GANs

1. **Balance Training:** Ensure generator and discriminator losses are balanced.
2. **Use Batch Normalization:** Helps stabilize training.
3. **Apply Regularization:** Prevents overfitting in the discriminator.
4. **Leverage Pre-Trained Models:** Use pre-trained discriminators for complex tasks.
5. **Experiment with Architectures:** Try variations like cGANs or WGANs for better performance.

---

8. Challenges with GANs

- **Mode Collapse:** Generator produces limited diversity.

- **Training Instability:** Adversarial training can be sensitive to hyperparameters.

- **Evaluation Metrics:** No standard metric for assessing GAN performance.

Generative Adversarial Networks are a groundbreaking advancement in generative modeling. With applications ranging from image generation to style transfer, GANs have become an essential tool in AI. By mastering their architecture and implementation, you can harness their potential to solve complex generative tasks effectively.

Chapter 22: Reinforcement Learning Basics

Overview

Reinforcement Learning (RL) is a branch of machine learning where agents learn to make decisions by interacting with an environment to maximize cumulative rewards. Unlike supervised learning, RL doesn't require labeled data but instead uses a reward-based system to guide the agent's actions.

---

1. What is Reinforcement Learning?

Key Concepts:

1. **Agent:** The decision-maker (e.g., a robot, game bot).
2. **Environment:** The world with which the agent interacts.
3. **State (sss):** A representation of the environment at a given time.
4. **Action (aaa):** A choice made by the agent.
5. **Reward (rrr):** Feedback from the environment for an action.
6. **Policy (π\pi$\pi$):** A strategy that maps states to actions.
7. **Value Function (V(s)V(s)V(s)):** Expected reward from a state when following a policy.

---

2. The RL Workflow

Steps in Reinforcement Learning:

1. **Initialization:** Define the environment and agent.
2. **State Observation:** Agent observes the current state.
3. **Action Selection:** Agent selects an action based on its policy.
4. **Environment Response:** Environment transitions to a new state and provides a reward.
5. **Policy Update:** Agent updates its policy to improve future decisions.

---

3. Types of RL Approaches

1. Model-Free vs. Model-Based:

- **Model-Free:** Learns directly from environment interactions without understanding its dynamics (e.g., Q-learning, Policy Gradient).
- **Model-Based:** Builds a model of the environment and uses it to plan actions.

2. Value-Based vs. Policy-Based:

- **Value-Based:** Learns a value function (e.g., Q-learning).

- **Policy-Based:** Directly learns the policy (e.g., Policy Gradient).

3. On-Policy vs. Off-Policy:

- **On-Policy:** Learns the value of the policy being executed (e.g., SARSA).
- **Off-Policy:** Learns the value of an optimal policy, even if another policy is followed (e.g., Q-learning).

---

4. Markov Decision Process (MDP)

RL problems are often framed as a **Markov Decision Process (MDP):**

1. **States (SSS):** Set of possible states.
2. **Actions (AAA):** Set of possible actions.
3. **Transition Function $(P(s'|s,a)P(s'|s,a)P(s'|s,a))$:** Probability of transitioning to state $s's's'$ given state sss and action aaa.
4. **Reward Function $(R(s,a)R(s,a)R(s,a))$:** Immediate reward for taking action aaa in state sss.

---

5. Q-Learning

What is Q-Learning?

Q-learning is a value-based method where the agent learns an action-value function $Q(s,a)Q(s, a)Q(s,a)$, which predicts the expected cumulative reward of taking action aaa in state sss and following the optimal policy thereafter.

Update Rule:

$Q(s,a)=Q(s,a)+\alpha(r+\gamma\max_{a'}Q(s',a')-Q(s,a))Q(s, a) = Q(s, a) + \alpha \left(r + \gamma \max_{a'} Q(s', a') - Q(s, a) \right)Q(s,a)=Q(s,a)+\alpha(r+\gamma a'\max Q(s',a')-Q(s,a))$

Where:

- $\alpha\alpha$: Learning rate.
- $\gamma\gamma$: Discount factor.
- rrr: Immediate reward.
- $s's's'$: Next state.

Q-Learning Example in Python:

1. Import Libraries:

python

import numpy as np

2. Initialize Environment and Q-Table:

python

```python
# Example: Grid world with 4 states and 2 actions
states = 4
actions = 2
q_table = np.zeros((states, actions))

# Hyperparameters
learning_rate = 0.1
discount_factor = 0.9
epsilon = 0.1  # Exploration probability
```

3. Simulate Agent Interaction:

python

```python
for episode in range(100):
    state = np.random.randint(0, states)  # Start in a random state
    for step in range(50):
        # Epsilon-greedy action selection
        if np.random.rand() < epsilon:
            action = np.random.randint(0, actions)
        else:
            action = np.argmax(q_table[state])

        # Simulate environment response
        next_state = (state + action) % states  # Example transition
        reward = 1 if next_state == 3 else 0  # Reward for reaching state 3

        # Q-Learning update
        q_table[state, action] += learning_rate * (
            reward + discount_factor * np.max(q_table[next_state]) - q_table[state,
action]
```

```
)
```

```
state = next_state  # Move to next state
```

4. Result:

python

```
print("Trained Q-Table:")
print(q_table)
```

---

6. Deep Reinforcement Learning (Deep Q-Learning)

Why Deep Q-Learning?

For complex environments with large state spaces (e.g., video games), using a Q-table becomes infeasible. Deep Q-Learning replaces the Q-table with a neural network that approximates $Q(s,a)Q(s, a)Q(s,a)$.

Key Innovations:

1. **Experience Replay:** Store agent experiences and sample them randomly for training.
2. **Target Network:** Use a separate network to stabilize updates.

Deep Q-Learning Example:

1. Import Libraries:

python

```
import tensorflow as tf
import numpy as np
```

2. Define the Q-Network:

python

```
model = tf.keras.Sequential([
    tf.keras.layers.Dense(24, activation="relu", input_shape=(state_space,)),
    tf.keras.layers.Dense(24, activation="relu"),
    tf.keras.layers.Dense(action_space, activation="linear")
])
model.compile(optimizer="adam", loss="mse")
```

3. Training Loop:

python

```
# Initialize variables
epsilon = 1.0  # Exploration rate
epsilon_decay = 0.995
min_epsilon = 0.01

for episode in range(1000):
    state = env.reset()  # Reset environment
    state = np.reshape(state, [1, state_space])
    total_reward = 0

    for step in range(200):
        # Epsilon-greedy action selection
```

```
if np.random.rand() < epsilon:
    action = np.random.randint(0, action_space)
else:
    action = np.argmax(model.predict(state))

# Take action and observe result
next_state, reward, done, _ = env.step(action)
next_state = np.reshape(next_state, [1, state_space])

# Store experience
memory.append((state, action, reward, next_state, done))

# Train model using experience replay
if len(memory) > batch_size:
    minibatch = random.sample(memory, batch_size)
    for s, a, r, ns, d in minibatch:
        target = r
        if not d:
            target += gamma * np.amax(model.predict(ns))
        target_f = model.predict(s)
        target_f[0][a] = target
        model.fit(s, target_f, epochs=1, verbose=0)

state = next_state
total_reward += reward
if done:
    break

# Reduce exploration rate
epsilon = max(min_epsilon, epsilon * epsilon_decay)
```

7. Applications of Reinforcement Learning

1. **Game Playing:** AlphaGo, Dota 2 bots, Atari games.
2. **Robotics:** Path planning, manipulation tasks.
3. **Autonomous Vehicles:** Traffic navigation and decision-making.
4. **Finance:** Portfolio optimization and trading strategies.
5. **Healthcare:** Personalized treatment recommendations.

8. Best Practices for RL

1. **Reward Shaping:** Design appropriate reward signals to guide learning.
2. **Hyperparameter Tuning:** Experiment with learning rates, discount factors, and exploration strategies.
3. **Monitor Overfitting:** Use diverse environments or tasks to avoid overfitting to a specific scenario.

Reinforcement Learning is a powerful framework for solving sequential decision-making problems. From Q-learning to Deep Q-Networks, RL techniques provide agents with the ability to learn complex behaviors in dynamic environments, driving advancements in AI applications like gaming, robotics, and autonomous systems.

Chapter 23: AI for Computer Vision

Overview

Computer Vision enables machines to interpret and process visual data from the world, mimicking human vision. With advancements in AI, tasks like face recognition, medical imaging, object detection, and autonomous driving have become achievable. This chapter delves into advanced AI applications for Computer Vision, focusing on face recognition and medical imaging.

---

1. What is Computer Vision?

Definition:

Computer Vision is a field of AI that trains computers to interpret and analyze visual data (images or videos).

Core Tasks in Computer Vision:

1. **Image Classification:** Categorizing images into predefined classes.
2. **Object Detection:** Identifying objects and their locations in an image.
3. **Segmentation:** Dividing images into meaningful parts (e.g., foreground vs. background).

4. **Facial Recognition:** Identifying or verifying individuals from facial features.

5. **Medical Imaging:** Detecting anomalies in X-rays, MRIs, or CT scans.

---

2. Key Technologies in Computer Vision

1. Convolutional Neural Networks (CNNs):

- Backbone of most Computer Vision tasks.
- Extract hierarchical features from images.

2. Pre-Trained Models:

- **ResNet:** For image classification and feature extraction.
- **YOLO (You Only Look Once):** Real-time object detection.
- **UNet:** Widely used in medical image segmentation.

3. Transfer Learning:
Using pre-trained models on large datasets (e.g., ImageNet) and fine-tuning them for specific tasks.

---

3. Advanced Application 1: Face Recognition

1. Pipeline for Face Recognition:

1. **Face Detection:** Locate faces in an image.

   o   Example models: Haar cascades, MTCNN.

2. **Feature Extraction:** Extract embeddings representing unique facial features.

   o   Example models: FaceNet, DeepFace.

3. **Face Matching:** Compare embeddings for identification or verification.

2. Implementation:

1. Face Detection with MTCNN:

python

```python
from mtcnn import MTCNN
import cv2

# Load image
image = cv2.imread("face.jpg")
detector = MTCNN()

# Detect faces
faces = detector.detect_faces(image)
for face in faces:
    x, y, width, height = face["box"]
    cv2.rectangle(image, (x, y), (x+width, y+height), (255, 0, 0), 2)

cv2.imshow("Faces", image)
cv2.waitKey(0)
```

2. Face Recognition with FaceNet:

python

```python
from keras.models import load_model
import numpy as np

# Load FaceNet model
model = load_model("facenet_keras.h5")

# Preprocess image
def preprocess_image(image):
    image = cv2.resize(image, (160, 160))
    image = np.expand_dims(image, axis=0)
    return image / 255.0

# Extract embedding
image = preprocess_image(cv2.imread("face.jpg"))
embedding = model.predict(image)
print("Face Embedding:", embedding)
```

3. *Applications of Face Recognition:*

- Security systems and biometric authentication.
- Social media tagging (e.g., Facebook).
- Smart home devices (e.g., Google Nest, Amazon Echo).

4. Advanced Application 2: Medical Imaging

1. Importance of AI in Medical Imaging:

- Improves diagnostic accuracy.
- Reduces workload for radiologists.
- Enables early detection of diseases (e.g., cancer, COVID-19).

2. Tasks in Medical Imaging:

1. **Segmentation:** Delineating anatomical structures or abnormalities.
   - Example: Segmenting tumors in MRI scans.
2. **Classification:** Identifying disease presence.
   - Example: Detecting pneumonia in X-rays.
3. **Detection:** Localizing abnormalities.
   - Example: Highlighting fractures in CT scans.

3. Implementation:

1. Image Classification Example (Pneumonia Detection):

python

```
import tensorflow as tf
from tensorflow.keras.models import Sequential
from tensorflow.keras.layers import Conv2D, MaxPooling2D, Flatten, Dense, Dropout
from tensorflow.keras.preprocessing.image import ImageDataGenerator

# Data Augmentation
```

```python
train_datagen   =   ImageDataGenerator(rescale=1./255,   rotation_range=20,
zoom_range=0.2, horizontal_flip=True)
train_data = train_datagen.flow_from_directory("train_data", target_size=(224,
224), class_mode="binary")

# Model
model = Sequential([
    Conv2D(32, (3, 3), activation="relu", input_shape=(224, 224, 3)),
    MaxPooling2D((2, 2)),
    Conv2D(64, (3, 3), activation="relu"),
    MaxPooling2D((2, 2)),
    Flatten(),
    Dense(128, activation="relu"),
    Dropout(0.5),
    Dense(1, activation="sigmoid")
])

model.compile(optimizer="adam",                loss="binary_crossentropy",
metrics=["accuracy"])
model.fit(train_data, epochs=10, batch_size=32)
```

2. Tumor Segmentation with UNet:

python

```python
from   tensorflow.keras.layers   import   Input,   Conv2D,   MaxPooling2D,
UpSampling2D, concatenate
from tensorflow.keras.models import Model

# UNet Model
def unet_model(input_size=(256, 256, 1)):
    inputs = Input(input_size)
```

```
conv1 = Conv2D(64, 3, activation="relu", padding="same")(inputs)
pool1 = MaxPooling2D(pool_size=(2, 2))(conv1)
conv2 = Conv2D(128, 3, activation="relu", padding="same")(pool1)
pool2 = MaxPooling2D(pool_size=(2, 2))(conv2)

up1 = UpSampling2D(size=(2, 2))(pool2)
merge1 = concatenate([conv2, up1], axis=3)
conv3 = Conv2D(64, 3, activation="relu", padding="same")(merge1)
outputs = Conv2D(1, 1, activation="sigmoid")(conv3)

model = Model(inputs=inputs, outputs=outputs)
return model

model = unet_model()
model.compile(optimizer="adam",                    loss="binary_crossentropy",
metrics=["accuracy"])
```

4. Applications of Medical Imaging:

- **Radiology:** Detection of fractures, tumors, and lesions.
- **Cardiology:** Segmentation of heart chambers in echocardiograms.
- **Ophthalmology:** Diagnosis of diabetic retinopathy.

---

5. Challenges in Computer Vision Applications

1. **Data Quality:** Poor quality or limited labeled datasets can impact performance.

2. **Interpretability:** Ensuring model predictions are explainable for critical applications like healthcare.

3. **Computational Costs:** Large models and datasets require significant resources.

4. **Ethics and Privacy:** Handling sensitive data like facial images or medical scans responsibly.

6. Best Practices

1. **Use Pre-Trained Models:** Leverage architectures like ResNet, UNet, and YOLO for faster development.

2. **Data Augmentation:** Enhance dataset diversity with rotation, cropping, and flipping.

3. **Transfer Learning:** Fine-tune models pre-trained on large datasets (e.g., ImageNet).

4. **Evaluation Metrics:** Use metrics like precision, recall, F1-score, and ROC-AUC for performance assessment.

AI-powered Computer Vision is transforming industries by automating and improving visual data analysis. Applications like face recognition and medical imaging demonstrate the versatility and potential of AI to address complex challenges. With the right tools and techniques, Computer Vision systems can achieve remarkable accuracy and efficiency in solving real-world problems.

Chapter 24: AI for Recommendation Systems

Overview

Recommendation systems use AI to suggest relevant items to users based on their preferences or behavior. These systems are widely used in e-commerce, streaming platforms, and social media. This chapter explores the core techniques of recommendation systems, including **collaborative filtering**, **content-based filtering**, and **hybrid models**.

---

1. What is a Recommendation System?

Definition:

A recommendation system predicts a user's preference for items and suggests relevant products, content, or services.

Types of Recommendation Systems:

1. **Collaborative Filtering:** Relies on user-item interactions.
2. **Content-Based Filtering:** Uses item features and user preferences.
3. **Hybrid Models:** Combines collaborative and content-based methods.

Applications:

- **E-commerce:** Suggesting products (e.g., Amazon).
- **Streaming Services:** Recommending movies or music (e.g., Netflix, Spotify).
- **Social Media:** Suggesting connections, posts, or groups (e.g., LinkedIn, Facebook).

---

2. Collaborative Filtering

Definition:

Collaborative filtering recommends items based on the interactions of users with similar preferences.

Types of Collaborative Filtering:

1. **User-Based:** Finds similar users and recommends items they liked.
2. **Item-Based:** Finds similar items based on user interactions and recommends them.

Matrix Factorization for Collaborative Filtering:

Matrix factorization decomposes the user-item interaction matrix into lower-dimensional representations of users and items.

$R = U \cdot I^T$

Where:

- RRR: User-item interaction matrix.
- UUU: User latent feature matrix.
- III: Item latent feature matrix.

Example: Collaborative Filtering with Matrix Factorization

1. Import Libraries:

python

```python
import numpy as np
from sklearn.decomposition import TruncatedSVD
```

2. Create User-Item Matrix:

python

```python
# Example user-item matrix
ratings = np.array([
    [5, 3, 0, 1],
    [4, 0, 0, 1],
    [1, 1, 0, 5],
    [1, 0, 0, 4],
    [0, 1, 5, 4],
])

# Fill missing values (optional)
ratings[ratings == 0] = np.mean(ratings[ratings != 0])
```

3. Perform Matrix Factorization:

python

```
svd = TruncatedSVD(n_components=2)  # Reduce to 2 latent features
user_features = svd.fit_transform(ratings)
item_features = svd.components_.T

# Predicted ratings
predicted_ratings = np.dot(user_features, item_features.T)
print(predicted_ratings)
```

---

3. Content-Based Filtering

Definition:

Content-based filtering recommends items based on their features and the user's preferences.

Steps:

1. Represent items as feature vectors.
2. Compute similarity between items and the user's history.
3. Recommend the most similar items.

Example: Movie Recommendation

1. Import Libraries:

python

```
from sklearn.feature_extraction.text import TfidfVectorizer
```

```
from sklearn.metrics.pairwise import cosine_similarity
```

2. Create Item Features:

python

```python
movies = ["Action movie with superheroes", "Romantic comedy", "Documentary on nature"]
user_preference = "I love superhero action movies"

# Convert text to vectors
vectorizer = TfidfVectorizer()
movie_features = vectorizer.fit_transform(movies)
user_vector = vectorizer.transform([user_preference])
```

3. Compute Similarity:

python

```python
similarity = cosine_similarity(user_vector, movie_features)
print("Similarity Scores:", similarity)
recommended_index = similarity.argmax()
print("Recommended Movie:", movies[recommended_index])
```

---

4. Hybrid Models

Definition:

Hybrid models combine collaborative and content-based methods to leverage the strengths of both approaches.

Techniques for Hybrid Models:

1. Combine predictions from collaborative and content-based systems.
2. Use content-based features as input to collaborative filtering.
3. Use collaborative filtering to initialize content-based models.

Example: Weighted Hybrid System

1. Define Ratings and Features:

python

```
collaborative_scores = np.array([0.8, 0.6, 0.3])  # From collaborative filtering
content_based_scores = np.array([0.7, 0.8, 0.4])  # From content-based filtering

# Assign weights to each system
collaborative_weight = 0.6
content_weight = 0.4
```

2. Compute Hybrid Scores:

python

```
hybrid_scores = (collaborative_weight * collaborative_scores) + (content_weight * content_based_scores)
print("Hybrid Scores:", hybrid_scores)

recommended_index = hybrid_scores.argmax()
print("Recommended Item Index:", recommended_index)
```

---

5. Deep Learning for Recommendation Systems

Neural Collaborative Filtering:

Uses neural networks to model interactions between users and items.

Example: Deep Collaborative Filtering

python

```python
import tensorflow as tf
from tensorflow.keras.models import Model
from tensorflow.keras.layers import Embedding, Flatten, Input, Dot

# Define inputs
user_input = Input(shape=(1,))
item_input = Input(shape=(1,))

# Embeddings
user_embedding = Embedding(input_dim=1000, output_dim=50)(user_input)
item_embedding = Embedding(input_dim=1000, output_dim=50)(item_input)

# Flatten and dot product
user_vec = Flatten()(user_embedding)
item_vec = Flatten()(item_embedding)
dot_product = Dot(axes=1)([user_vec, item_vec])

# Build model
model = Model(inputs=[user_input, item_input], outputs=dot_product)
model.compile(optimizer="adam", loss="mse")
model.summary()
```

6. Evaluation Metrics

Metrics for Recommendation Systems:

1. **Precision@K:** Proportion of relevant items in the top KKK recommendations.
2. **Recall@K:** Proportion of relevant items retrieved out of all relevant items.
3. **F1 Score:** Harmonic mean of precision and recall.
4. **Mean Absolute Error (MAE):** Measures the average error in predicted ratings.

---

7. Challenges in Recommendation Systems

1. **Cold Start Problem:**
   - **User Cold Start:** New users lack interaction history.
   - **Item Cold Start:** New items have no user ratings.

   Solution: Use content-based or hybrid methods.

2. **Scalability:**
   - Large datasets require efficient algorithms.
   - **Solution:** Use matrix factorization or distributed systems.

3. **Diversity vs. Accuracy:**

- o Balancing relevance and diversity in recommendations.

4. **Bias and Fairness:**
   - o Ensuring recommendations are unbiased and inclusive.

---

8. Best Practices

1. **Leverage Pre-Trained Models:** Use existing embeddings (e.g., word2vec for content-based models).
2. **Feature Engineering:** Extract meaningful features for both users and items.
3. **Regularization:** Prevent overfitting in collaborative filtering.
4. **Experiment with Hybrid Models:** Combine multiple techniques to achieve better performance.

Recommendation systems are essential in personalizing user experiences and driving engagement. By mastering collaborative filtering, content-based filtering, and hybrid models, you can build robust systems tailored to specific domains. Combining these techniques with deep learning can further enhance accuracy and scalability, enabling state-of-the-art recommendation systems.

Chapter 25: Explainable AI (XAI)

Overview

Explainable AI (XAI) aims to make AI models transparent, interpretable, and trustworthy. As AI systems are increasingly deployed in critical domains such as healthcare, finance, and criminal justice, the need for understanding their decision-making processes has become vital. This chapter explores the concepts, techniques, and applications of XAI in real-world scenarios.

---

1. What is Explainable AI (XAI)?

Definition:

Explainable AI refers to methods and techniques that enable humans to understand and trust the decisions made by AI models.

Goals of XAI:

1. **Transparency:** Clarify how models work and make predictions.
2. **Accountability:** Allow stakeholders to evaluate AI decisions.
3. **Trustworthiness:** Build confidence in AI systems by explaining their behavior.

Importance of XAI:

- Increases user trust and adoption of AI systems.
- Ensures compliance with regulations (e.g., GDPR's "right to explanation").
- Identifies and mitigates biases in models.

---

2. Challenges of Interpretability

1. **Complexity of Models:**
   - Advanced models like neural networks are often considered "black boxes."
   - Hard to understand relationships between inputs and outputs.

2. **Trade-Off Between Accuracy and Interpretability:**
   - Simpler models (e.g., decision trees) are more interpretable but may sacrifice accuracy compared to complex models.

3. **Bias and Ethical Concerns:**
   - Ensuring explanations are not only interpretable but also unbiased and fair.

---

3. Types of Interpretability

1. Intrinsic Interpretability:

Models that are inherently interpretable due to their simplicity, such as:

- Decision Trees
- Linear Regression
- Rule-Based Models

2. Post-Hoc Interpretability:

Techniques applied after model training to explain predictions, including:

- Feature importance
- Partial dependence plots
- Local explanations (e.g., LIME, SHAP)

---

4. Techniques for XAI

1. Feature Importance:

Ranks features based on their contribution to model predictions.

Example: Feature Importance in Random Forest

python

```
from sklearn.ensemble import RandomForestClassifier
from sklearn.datasets import load_iris
```

Load data

```
data = load_iris()
X, y = data.data, data.target

# Train model
model = RandomForestClassifier()
model.fit(X, y)

# Get feature importance
importances = model.feature_importances_
for feature, importance in zip(data.feature_names, importances):
    print(f"{feature}: {importance}")
```

---

2. Partial Dependence Plots (PDPs):

Visualize the relationship between a feature and the predicted outcome while marginalizing other features.

Example: PDP with Scikit-Learn

python

```
from sklearn.inspection import plot_partial_dependence
import matplotlib.pyplot as plt

# Partial dependence plot
plot_partial_dependence(model, X, [0], feature_names=data.feature_names)
plt.show()
```

---

3. LIME (Local Interpretable Model-Agnostic Explanations):

LIME explains individual predictions by approximating the complex model with an interpretable one locally around a specific instance.

Example: LIME Implementation

python

```
from lime.lime_tabular import LimeTabularExplainer

# Initialize explainer
explainer          =          LimeTabularExplainer(X,          training_labels=y,
feature_names=data.feature_names, class_names=data.target_names)

# Explain prediction
explanation = explainer.explain_instance(X[0], model.predict_proba)
explanation.show_in_notebook()
```

---

4. SHAP (SHapley Additive exPlanations):

SHAP assigns a contribution value to each feature, explaining its impact on the prediction.

Example: SHAP Implementation

python

```
import shap

# Initialize explainer
explainer = shap.TreeExplainer(model)
shap_values = explainer.shap_values(X)
```

```
# Visualize explanations
shap.summary_plot(shap_values, X, feature_names=data.feature_names)
```

---

5. Surrogate Models:

Train a simpler, interpretable model (e.g., decision tree) to mimic the predictions of a complex model.

---

5. Applications of XAI

1. Healthcare:

- **Example:** AI predicts disease diagnosis.
- XAI ensures clinicians understand why the model suggests specific outcomes, enabling better trust and adoption.

2. Finance:

- **Example:** Loan approval systems.
- XAI explains why a loan was approved or denied, ensuring transparency and fairness.

3. Autonomous Systems:

- **Example:** Self-driving cars.

- XAI explains actions like braking or turning, ensuring safety and accountability.

4. *Legal and Criminal Justice:*

- **Example:** Recidivism prediction tools.
- XAI ensures models comply with fairness and avoid discrimination.

---

6. Best Practices for XAI

1. **Choose the Right Technique:**
   - Use simple, interpretable models if interpretability is critical.
   - Apply post-hoc techniques for complex models.
2. **Involve Stakeholders:**
   - Collaborate with domain experts to ensure explanations align with user needs.
3. **Test for Bias:**
   - Regularly evaluate explanations for potential biases in data or model behavior.
4. **Integrate into Workflows:**
   - Ensure explanations are actionable and useful for end-users.

7. Limitations of XAI

1. **Scalability:**
   - o Some interpretability techniques (e.g., LIME) may be computationally expensive for large datasets.

2. **Human Interpretability:**
   - o Explanations may still be too technical for non-expert users.

3. **Potential for Misinterpretation:**
   - o Explanations might oversimplify or misrepresent the model's behavior.

Explainable AI bridges the gap between model accuracy and user trust by providing transparent, interpretable insights into AI decision-making. From techniques like SHAP and LIME to real-world applications in healthcare and finance, XAI is essential for building trustworthy AI systems. Mastering XAI enables developers to create models that are not only accurate but also ethical, fair, and transparent.

Chapter 26: Deploying AI Models

Overview

Deployment is the final stage of the AI lifecycle, where a trained model is made accessible to end-users. Packaging and deploying models allow applications to leverage AI predictions in real-time or batch processing. This chapter focuses on deploying AI models using **Flask**, **FastAPI**, and **Docker**, covering practical steps and best practices.

---

1. Importance of AI Model Deployment

Why Deploy AI Models?

1. **Real-Time Predictions:** Enable applications to use models for live decision-making (e.g., chatbots, fraud detection).
2. **Scalability:** Serve multiple users or systems simultaneously.
3. **Automation:** Integrate predictions into existing workflows or systems.

Common Deployment Scenarios:

- **Web Applications:** Embedding models in web-based tools.
- **APIs:** Providing model predictions as services.

- **Edge Devices:** Deploying lightweight models for IoT and mobile devices.

---

2. Packaging Models for Deployment

1. Save the Trained Model:

Most frameworks allow saving trained models for reuse.

Example with Scikit-Learn:

python

```
from sklearn.externals import joblib

# Train and save model
joblib.dump(model, "model.pkl")

# Load model
model = joblib.load("model.pkl")
```

Example with TensorFlow/Keras:

python

```
# Save model
model.save("model.h5")

# Load model
from tensorflow.keras.models import load_model
model = load_model("model.h5")
```

3. Deployment with Flask

What is Flask?

Flask is a lightweight Python web framework suitable for creating APIs to serve AI models.

Steps for Flask Deployment:

1. Install Flask:

bash

```
pip install flask
```

2. Create Flask App:

python

```
from flask import Flask, request, jsonify
import joblib

# Load model
model = joblib.load("model.pkl")

app = Flask(__name__)

@app.route('/predict', methods=['POST'])
def predict():
    data = request.get_json()  # Get input data
    prediction = model.predict([data['features']])
```

```
return jsonify({'prediction': prediction.tolist()})
```

```
if __name__ == "__main__":
    app.run(debug=True)
```

3. Run the App:

bash

```
python app.py
```

4. Test the API:

Using curl or Postman:

bash

```
curl -X POST -H "Content-Type: application/json" -d '{"features": [1, 2, 3, 4]}' http://127.0.0.1:5000/predict
```

---

4. Deployment with FastAPI

What is FastAPI?

FastAPI is a modern web framework that supports asynchronous operations and automatic API documentation with **Swagger**.

Steps for FastAPI Deployment:

1. Install FastAPI and Uvicorn:

bash

```
pip install fastapi uvicorn
```

2. Create FastAPI App:

python

```python
from fastapi import FastAPI
from pydantic import BaseModel
import joblib

# Load model
model = joblib.load("model.pkl")

# Define input schema
class InputData(BaseModel):
    features: list

app = FastAPI()

@app.post("/predict")
async def predict(data: InputData):
    prediction = model.predict([data.features])
    return {"prediction": prediction.tolist()}
```

3. Run the App:

bash

```bash
uvicorn app:app --reload
```

4. Test the API:

Access http://127.0.0.1:8000/docs for Swagger-based API documentation and testing.

5. Containerization with Docker

Why Use Docker?

Docker allows you to package your application and dependencies into a container, ensuring consistency across different environments.

Steps for Dockerizing an AI Application:

1. Install Docker:

Follow the installation guide for your platform: Docker Installation.

2. Create a Dockerfile:

dockerfile

```
# Use Python base image
FROM python:3.9

# Set working directory
WORKDIR /app

# Copy files
COPY requirements.txt .
COPY app.py .

# Install dependencies
RUN pip install -r requirements.txt

# Expose port
```

EXPOSE 5000

Run the Flask app
CMD ["python", "app.py"]

3. Build the Docker Image:

bash

docker build -t ai-model-deployment .

4. Run the Container:

bash

docker run -p 5000:5000 ai-model-deployment

5. Test the API:

Use the same curl or Postman request as before, but replace the URL with your container's address.

---

6. Deployment Best Practices

1. Use a Reverse Proxy:

Deploy behind a reverse proxy like **Nginx** or **Apache** for better performance and security.

2. Add Logging and Monitoring:

Monitor model predictions, response times, and errors using tools like **Prometheus** or **ELK Stack**.

3. Optimize for Scalability:

Use cloud-based services like AWS, Azure, or Google Cloud to scale your API with load balancers.

4. Secure the API:

- Use HTTPS for secure communication.
- Add authentication mechanisms like API keys or OAuth.

5. Enable Model Versioning:

Track and deploy specific versions of your model for updates or rollback.

---

7. Real-World Deployment Example

Deploying on AWS Lambda:

1. Export the model and dependencies as a ZIP file.
2. Write a Lambda function to load the model and handle requests.
3. Use **Amazon API Gateway** to expose the Lambda function as an API.

Deploying on Google Cloud Run:

1. Package the application with a Dockerfile.
2. Push the Docker image to **Google Container Registry**.

3. Deploy the container on **Google Cloud Run** for serverless execution.

Deploying AI models is a critical step to transforming prototypes into real-world applications. Flask and FastAPI provide lightweight frameworks for creating APIs, while Docker ensures portability and consistency. By following best practices, you can deploy robust, scalable, and secure AI systems to serve predictions in production environments effectively.

Chapter 27: End-to-End AI Project: Predicting Customer Churn

Overview

Customer churn prediction is a critical task for businesses aiming to retain customers and optimize revenue. In this hands-on project, you will build and deploy an end-to-end AI system to predict customer churn, covering data preprocessing, model training, evaluation, and deployment using Flask.

---

1. Understanding Customer Churn Prediction

What is Customer Churn?

Customer churn occurs when a customer stops using a company's products or services. Predicting churn allows businesses to take proactive measures to retain customers.

Project Workflow:

1. **Data Collection:** Obtain customer data with relevant features.
2. **Data Preprocessing:** Clean and prepare data for modeling.
3. **Model Training:** Build and train a predictive model.
4. **Evaluation:** Measure model performance.
5. **Deployment:** Deploy the model as a REST API.

2. Data Collection and Preprocessing

Step 1: Import Libraries

python

```
import pandas as pd
import numpy as np
from sklearn.model_selection import train_test_split
from sklearn.preprocessing import LabelEncoder, StandardScaler
```

Step 2: Load Dataset

python

```
# Load customer churn dataset
data = pd.read_csv('customer_churn.csv')
print(data.head())
```

Step 3: Data Cleaning

python

```
# Check for missing values
data.isnull().sum()

# Fill or drop missing values
data.fillna(method='ffill', inplace=True)
```

Step 4: Feature Encoding

python

```python
# Encode categorical variables
label_encoders = {}
for column in ['Gender', 'Geography']:
    le = LabelEncoder()
    data[column] = le.fit_transform(data[column])
    label_encoders[column] = le
```

Step 5: Feature Scaling

python

```python
# Scale numerical features
scaler = StandardScaler()
scaled_features = scaler.fit_transform(data[['CreditScore', 'Age', 'Balance']])
data[['CreditScore', 'Age', 'Balance']] = scaled_features
```

Step 6: Split Data

python

```python
X = data.drop('Exited', axis=1)  # Features
y = data['Exited']  # Target variable

X_train, X_test, y_train, y_test = train_test_split(X, y, test_size=0.2, random_state=42)
```

---

3. Model Training

Step 1: Train a Model

python

```python
from sklearn.ensemble import RandomForestClassifier
```

```
from sklearn.metrics import accuracy_score, classification_report
```

```
# Train model
model = RandomForestClassifier(n_estimators=100, random_state=42)
model.fit(X_train, y_train)
```

```
# Make predictions
y_pred = model.predict(X_test)
```

Step 2: Evaluate the Model
python

```
# Evaluate performance
accuracy = accuracy_score(y_test, y_pred)
print(f"Accuracy: {accuracy}")
print(classification_report(y_test, y_pred))
```

---

4. Deployment with Flask

Step 1: Save the Model
python

```
import joblib
```

```
# Save trained model and scaler
joblib.dump(model, 'churn_model.pkl')
joblib.dump(scaler, 'scaler.pkl')
```

Step 2: Create a Flask App
python

```python
from flask import Flask, request, jsonify
import joblib
import numpy as np

# Load model and scaler
model = joblib.load('churn_model.pkl')
scaler = joblib.load('scaler.pkl')

app = Flask(__name__)

@app.route('/predict', methods=['POST'])
def predict():
    # Get input data
    data = request.get_json()
    features = np.array(data['features']).reshape(1, -1)
    scaled_features = scaler.transform(features)

    # Predict churn
    prediction = model.predict(scaled_features)
    return jsonify({'churn': int(prediction[0])})

if __name__ == '__main__':
    app.run(debug=True)
```

Step 3: Test the API

bash

```bash
curl -X POST -H "Content-Type: application/json" -d '{"features": [600, 40, 0, 1, 1, 100000]}' http://127.0.0.1:5000/predict
```

5. Enhancing the Model

Feature Importance Analysis

python

```python
import matplotlib.pyplot as plt

# Plot feature importance
importances = model.feature_importances_
features = X.columns
plt.barh(features, importances)
plt.xlabel('Importance')
plt.ylabel('Feature')
plt.show()
```

Hyperparameter Tuning

python

```python
from sklearn.model_selection import GridSearchCV

# Define parameter grid
param_grid = {
    'n_estimators': [50, 100, 200],
    'max_depth': [None, 10, 20],
}

# Perform grid search
```

```
grid_search    =    GridSearchCV(RandomForestClassifier(random_state=42),
param_grid, cv=5)
grid_search.fit(X_train, y_train)
print(grid_search.best_params_)
```

---

6. Scaling the Deployment

Containerizing with Docker

Step 1: Create a Dockerfile

dockerfile

```
FROM python:3.9
WORKDIR /app
COPY requirements.txt .
RUN pip install -r requirements.txt
COPY . .
EXPOSE 5000
CMD ["python", "app.py"]
```

Step 2: Build and Run the Container

bash

```
docker build -t churn-prediction .
docker run -p 5000:5000 churn-prediction
```

---

7. Monitoring and Maintenance

Monitoring:

- Use tools like **Prometheus** and **Grafana** to monitor API usage and model performance.

Model Retraining:

- Periodically update the model with new data to ensure it remains accurate.

This project demonstrates how to build and deploy an end-to-end AI system for predicting customer churn. By integrating data preprocessing, model training, evaluation, and deployment into a seamless pipeline, businesses can proactively address churn and enhance customer retention strategies. This approach can be scaled and customized for other predictive tasks.

Chapter 28: Final Capstone: AI for Social Good

Overview

AI for social good focuses on leveraging artificial intelligence to address pressing societal issues such as healthcare accessibility, environmental sustainability, disaster response, and education inequality. This capstone project demonstrates how to develop an AI system that solves a real-world societal problem, combining technical expertise with social impact.

---

1. Project Idea: Predicting Air Quality for Public Health

Objective:

Develop an AI system that predicts air quality and provides actionable insights to reduce pollution exposure and improve public health.

Scope:

- Predict Air Quality Index (AQI) using real-time environmental data.
- Provide recommendations for reducing pollution exposure.
- Serve predictions through a web-based dashboard.

2. Workflow

1. **Data Collection:**
   - Collect historical air quality and weather data from sources like OpenWeather API and EPA Air Quality API.

2. **Data Preprocessing:**
   - Clean and prepare data, handle missing values, and engineer features.

3. **Model Training:**
   - Train a regression model to predict AQI based on input features.

4. **Deployment:**
   - Serve predictions via a web dashboard using Flask.

5. **Actionable Insights:**
   - Provide recommendations based on predicted AQI levels.

3. Data Collection

Step 1: Fetch Data

Use APIs to collect historical air quality and weather data.

python

```python
import requests
import pandas as pd

# Fetch data from OpenWeather API
api_key = "your_api_key"
url = f"http://api.openweathermap.org/data/2.5/air_pollution/history?lat=37.7749&lon=-122.4194&start=1638334800&end=1638929600&appid={api_key}"
response = requests.get(url)
data = response.json()

# Convert to DataFrame
df = pd.json_normalize(data['list'])
print(df.head())
```

Step 2: Save Data

Save the collected data locally or in a cloud storage bucket for preprocessing and model training.

python

```python
df.to_csv('air_quality_data.csv', index=False)
```

---

4. Data Preprocessing

Step 1: Handle Missing Values
python

```
# Fill missing values with column mean
df.fillna(df.mean(), inplace=True)
```

Step 2: Feature Engineering

Create features like:

- Temperature, humidity, and wind speed.
- Historical AQI values for time-series modeling.

python

```
df['month'] = pd.to_datetime(df['dt'], unit='s').dt.month
df['day'] = pd.to_datetime(df['dt'], unit='s').dt.day
```

5. Model Training

Step 1: Train-Test Split

python

```
from sklearn.model_selection import train_test_split

X = df[['temp', 'humidity', 'wind_speed', 'month', 'day']]
y = df['aqi']

X_train, X_test, y_train, y_test = train_test_split(X, y, test_size=0.2, random_state=42)
```

Step 2: Train a Regression Model

python

```python
from sklearn.ensemble import RandomForestRegressor
from sklearn.metrics import mean_squared_error

# Train model
model = RandomForestRegressor(n_estimators=100, random_state=42)
model.fit(X_train, y_train)

# Evaluate model
y_pred = model.predict(X_test)
print(f"Mean Squared Error: {mean_squared_error(y_test, y_pred)}")
```

Step 3: Save the Model

python

```python
import joblib
joblib.dump(model, 'aqi_model.pkl')
```

---

6. Deployment

Step 1: Create a Flask App

python

```python
from flask import Flask, request, jsonify
import joblib
import numpy as np

# Load model
```

```python
model = joblib.load('aqi_model.pkl')

app = Flask(__name__)

@app.route('/predict', methods=['POST'])
def predict():
    data = request.get_json()
    features = np.array(data['features']).reshape(1, -1)
    prediction = model.predict(features)
    return jsonify({'predicted_aqi': prediction[0]})

if __name__ == '__main__':
    app.run(debug=True)
```

Step 2: Test the API

bash

```bash
curl -X POST -H "Content-Type: application/json" -d '{"features": [15, 60, 3.5, 6, 15]}' http://127.0.0.1:5000/predict
```

---

7. Building a Dashboard

Step 1: Integrate Flask with Dash

Use Dash to build a user-friendly dashboard for visualizing AQI predictions and recommendations.

python

```python
from dash import Dash, dcc, html
```

```
import plotly.express as px
import pandas as pd

app = Dash(__name__)

# Load sample data
df = pd.read_csv('air_quality_data.csv')

# Create dashboard layout
app.layout = html.Div([
    html.H1("Air Quality Dashboard"),
    dcc.Graph(figure=px.line(df, x='date', y='aqi', title='AQI Over Time')),
])

if __name__ == '__main__':
    app.run_server(debug=True)
```

8. Recommendations for Public Health

Examples of Recommendations Based on AQI Levels:

- **Good (0-50):** "Air quality is good. No precautions necessary."
- **Moderate (51-100):** "Sensitive individuals should limit outdoor activities."
- **Unhealthy (101-150):** "Reduce prolonged outdoor exertion. Wear masks if needed."

- **Very Unhealthy (151-200):** "Avoid outdoor activities. Use air purifiers indoors."

---

9. Scaling and Monitoring

Scaling:

- Deploy the application on cloud platforms like **AWS**, **Azure**, or **Google Cloud**.
- Use Docker for containerization and Kubernetes for orchestration.

Monitoring:

- Monitor API usage and model performance using tools like **Prometheus** or **ELK Stack**.

---

10. Social Impact

Potential Benefits:

- Raise awareness about air pollution and its effects.
- Empower communities to take preventive measures.

- Provide actionable data to policymakers for environmental planning

This capstone project demonstrates how AI can be leveraged for social good by predicting air quality and improving public health outcomes. By combining data science, machine learning, and deployment techniques, this project provides a blueprint for addressing real-world societal challenges using AI.

www.ingramcontent.com/pod-product-compliance
Lightning Source LLC
LaVergne TN
LVHW051437050326
832903LV00030BD/3134